A SEASON WITH THE SAVIOR

A SEASON WITH THE SAVIOR

Meditations on Mark

EDWARD R. SIMS

A Crossroad Book
THE SEABURY PRESS • NEW YORK

1978
The Seabury Press
815 Second Avenue
New York, N.Y. 10017

Printed in the United States of America

Library of Congress Cataloging in Publication Data
Sims, Edward R.   A season with the Savior.
"A Crossroad book."
1. Bible. N.T. Mark—Meditations. 2. Lent—Prayer-
books and devotions—English. I. Title.
BS2585.4.S57   225'.3'06   78-18318
ISBN 0-8164-0413-5
ISBN 0-8164-2195-1 pbk.

PREFACE

The decade of the seventies has witnessed a rediscovery of conservative Christianity, and renewed attention to the Bible has been one of its happy and universal effects. Bible study groups have sprung up in the most unlikely places, attracting a wide variety of people to a new seriousness in Bible reading, a new confidence in the biblical revelation, and a new commitment to biblical truth. This book is meant to contribute to that process and to respond to the hunger it reveals.

The meditations cover Mark's Gospel and are arranged to occupy the forty days of Lent, including Sundays, with morning and evening readings for each day. The book offers one answer to the desire to make Lent a special season but is equally useful any time of the year. It is designed to help you cultivate the habit of daily nourishment from the Scriptures, the discipline of giving sufficient time to read through a book that speaks to you, and sufficient quiet to let the Spirit illumine and enlarge the words you have read.

The goal of such a nourishing discipline is a lively and growing personal relationship with Jesus Christ, a joyous sense of God's loving attention to your life and a sure trust in the power of the Spirit. Take a moment before each reading to compose yourself and to turn a receptive heart and mind to God; he will surely speak to you. As these periods of concentration on God's Word become more regular and consistent, your hearing will become more acute, I promise.

I urge the reader to keep at hand an easily read modern translation of the Gospel. Many good versions are available. I use the New English Bible in an edition I feel free to underline and annotate. My meditations supplement your reading of St. Mark; they are meant to make his narrative more real and fleshly and immediate to your life. The meditations are sequential, but you will discover some omissions and occasional overlapping. Mark's first twenty-two verses involve much introductory material and are given more detailed attention than the remainder of the Gospel.

After each Sunday's readings you will find a review of the preceding week and suggestions for discussion or reflection, designed particularly to assist in group study. The Sunday placement is arbitrary; the material is adaptable to any weekly use. I warmly commend group Bible study as a source of support and insight. Many kinds of group use are available: a Sunday group for this one purpose; a special series for a regularly meeting group; a neighborhood weekly gathering, perhaps with a contributive supper or a rotating host; a devotional addition to a group that gathers for a nonstudy purpose. Others will suggest themselves. The spirit of group discussion should be openness to God and to one another, and its atmosphere should afford freedom to each person to contribute his own personal response without needing to sound profound or to please the leader or build status. A rotating chairmanship often helps develop such an environment.

Whether in a group or alone, I urge readers to trust their own perceptions and understandings, to enter into them deeply and take time to think them through. The fruits of such prayerful study will seep out of the appointed times and into the larger consciousness of your day, where they will touch all that rich and varied fabric we call life and give it the joy and delight only Jesus can bring.

A preacher is privileged to share his pilgrimage with countless companions of every kind who, by their sophistication or their simplicity, enlighten and enrich his life. Their voices speak in the pages that follow and I cheerfully record my gratitude to them. I am grateful, as well, to those whose assistance and encouragement have made this book a reality and to you who accept me as a companion for a season. God be with us as we walk together.

EDWARD R. SIMS

FIRST WEEK

ASH WEDNESDAY MORNING
READING: MARK 1:1

"Here begins the Gospel of Jesus Christ the Son of God."

We will be reading St. Mark together these next forty days, and we'll cover all but a few verses in some detail.

It is the shortest, simplest, most direct of the Gospel accounts; its narrative bursts on us abruptly and carries us along in a kind of urgent rush. The story tumbles from Mark's pen faster than he can shape sentences, leaving a looseness of grammar that most translations tidy up. In his haste, he overuses the words translated "immediately," or "straightway," or "at the moment," but the effect is a heightened mood of excitement and importance.

Literal translations of Mark show that his Gospel opens with an incomplete sentence, and scholars have speculated that the early edition, which survived to become the standard, had lost its first and last pages. Those papyrus texts were made of long pages folded together in booklet form and held—where we would place a staple—by a leather thong or string. Frequently the outside sheet containing the first and last pages was torn away and disappeared. That may have happened to Mark, since the last sentence of the Gospel is also incomplete: ". . . for they were afraid of . . ."

Whatever its textual explanation, the incomplete sentence at the beginning starts the Gospel off at a run, a pace too urgent and breathless to bother with the niceties of grammar. Come along with me, and we'll see what Mark is so excited about.

Open our eyes, O God, to see you in your Son; open our hearts to follow where he leads.

ASH WEDNESDAY EVENING

READING: MARK 1:2–3

"In the prophet Isaiah it stands written: 'Here is my herald whom I send on ahead of you, and he will prepare your way. A voice crying aloud in the wilderness, "Prepare a way for the Lord; clear a straight path for him." ' "

At the very opening of his Gospel record, Mark makes it clear that its roots are in the Old Testament. Even more than that, he proclaims that the Gospel begins there, in the wisdom and vision of that ancient and perceptive people. Jesus himself confirms this in the course of his teaching; in countless places he echoes the language and the images of the Old Testament and many times, of course, quotes from it or refers directly to it.

One of our missionary arguments turns on the issue of the place of the Old Testament in nonwestern cultures and the degree to which indigenous sacred writings and traditions can replace it or supplement it. Before I was exposed to this controversy as a seminarian, I experienced it as a naval officer. The journey home from the Far East at the end of World War II took me to the island of Ceylon (now called Sri Lanka). A party of us spent a day in the city of Kandy and visited a notable Buddhist shrine there called The Temple of the Tooth. One of its exterior walls featured nine murals, depicting the nine hells of Buddhist tradition, one each for the punishment of a particular sin. I was struck by the close similarity to the Ten Commandments. The murals virtually duplicated that basic ethical statement. It was my first experience of the profound truth of monotheism.

We believe that God is everywhere at work and that wherever people reach out beyond themselves in thought, in behavior, or in wonder they are responding to God. We will probably argue endlessly about the necessity of the Old Testament in other cultures, but we can be sure of one thing: Wherever people respond to Jesus, God has already been at work.

Prepare in our hearts, Heavenly Father, the way of your coming; we turn to you in welcome and in hope.

THURSDAY MORNING
READING: MARK 1:4–5

"And so it was that John the Baptist appeared in the wilderness proclaiming a baptism in token of repentance, for the forgiveness of sins; and they flocked to him from the whole Judaean countryside and the city of Jerusalem, and were baptized by him in the River Jordan, confessing their sins."

Mark's talents at brevity are nowhere better displayed than in the fourth verse. There he has accomplished a one-clause summary of the core of John the Baptist's teachings: "A baptism in token of repentance for the forgiveness of sins." The chronological sequence is just the reverse of Mark's grammatical order: Forgiveness is God's act of love, repentance is our act of response, baptism is our act of declaration.

John was encouraging the baptism practiced in his time, a repeatable outward symbol of determination to change. We have made Holy Baptism the once-only sacrament of initiation into the Body of Christ and have never instituted a dramatic public rite of repentance, such as John seized upon. The baptism John preached did not create anything: it did not create the repentance nor did the repentance create God's forgiveness. The sequence is just the opposite: God's love creates repentance, the baptism proclaims repentance. This baptism is a token to seal and publish what has taken place in the heart: the response of repentance to the initiative of love.

Though we have no outward act of declaration like John's baptism, this is the sequence that feeds and sustains the Christian life: the daily claim of forgiveness by the daily act of repentance, a sequence that must be completed by some token. That token can be a prayer of thanks, a period of silence, an unspoken affirmation of peace. Love, response, token: This sacred sequence, which John proclaimed with such force and drama, still prepares the way for Christ.

Dear God, our minds are slow to believe what our hearts cry out for: a love quicker to listen than we to pray, readier to forgive than we to repent.

THURSDAY EVENING
READING: MARK 1:6–8

"John was dressed in a rough coat of camel's hair, with a leather belt round his waist, and he fed on locusts and wild honey. His proclamation ran: 'After me comes one who is mightier than I. I am not fit to unfasten his shoes. I have baptized you with water; he will baptize you with the Holy Spirit.'"

"After me comes one." This motto could be emblazoned on every Christian pulpit, it could stand over every Christian life. For the fact of the matter is that every Christian preacher points beyond himself, just as every Christian life points beyond itself.

I suppose there is really no other way the Christian church grows than by witness. It is inherent in every Christian calling and a part of every Christian act: In the very doing of it we proclaim something else, someone else. The focus is never on the Christian, except incidentally; the focus is on Christ. For all the emphasis we give to Christian behavior, its ultimate importance is not what it does but whom it reveals.

I have recently been reading a biography of Albert Schweitzer, that remarkable musician, theologian, and medical missionary. In speaking of his theological position, his biographer says of Schweitzer, "Others make their argument their life; Schweitzer made his life his argument." Everything about Schweitzer's life spoke of his conviction and everything about his life pointed beyond himself to God.

One of my seminary teachers, in speaking of Christian witness, compared it to the naturalness and ease with which one shares a sunset. We wouldn't think of failing to call it to the attention of someone nearby who hadn't noticed; that act of sharing—"look at that gorgeous sky!"—sharpens and deepens our own delight.

So with Christ; we cannot keep him to ourselves. And every act of witness imitates this ancient posture of John the Baptist, who comes with boldness and flair, not to achieve notoriety or to focus attention on himself, but to point to the one who comes after.

Fashion our lives, Heavenly Father, to point to Jesus; make our witness loving and unostentatious, but faithful and unashamed.

FRIDAY MORNING
READING: MARK 1:9–11

"It happened at this time that Jesus came from Nazareth in Galilee and was baptized in the Jordan by John. At the moment when he came up out of the water, he saw the heavens torn open and the Spirit, like a dove, descending upon him. And a voice spoke from heaven: 'Thou art my Son, my Beloved; on thee my favour rests.'"

It is curious how every act of God's that is a revelation always keeps something hidden. After receiving the tablets of the law, Moses pleaded with God to show him his face, to reveal himself entirely. But God directed Moses to hide in a cleft of rock, promising that as he passed by he would cover Moses' face with his hand, and Moses would see only where God had been, only the trail of glory he left behind. "No man," God tells Moses, "can look on the face of God and live."

So with this revelation Mark records after Jesus is baptized. The drama of signs and wonders is there—"The heavens were torn open"—but so is the darkness and the ambiguity. "Thou art my Son, my Beloved" or "Thou art my only Son"—we are left to wrestle with what it means. So every title given to Jesus is an attempt to express something about his uniqueness, something about his lordship, something about his power. But those titles are symbols, just as every word is a symbol, and the reality of Jesus' identity behind the symbols has occupied theologians, and common Christians like you and me, ever since this voice pierced the heavens.

Who is this Jesus? What has he to do with me? What difference does the Son of God make in my life? What power does he bring? Mark knows the episode leaves the questions, and so he writes a Gospel to give his answer.

You have claimed us as your own, dear God; stay close to us in the journey that lies ahead.

FRIDAY EVENING
READING: MARK 1:12–13

*"Thereupon the Spirit sent him away into the wilderness, and
there he remained for forty days tempted by Satan. He was
among the wild beasts; and the angels waited on him."*

Jesus went out into the wilderness after his own public declaration
of repentance, his own public claim on God's love. And those
wildernesses of the Near East are forbidding places: parched,
barren, empty, lifeless. A place of decision for Jesus, a time of
fateful consequence. Notice he was sent there, and sent by the
Spirit.

I have a friend who trains horses, and what he relishes most of
all is to find a young horse strong, energetic, and a little bit wild.
Such wildness he can shape and mold and redirect into a fine
gait, a noble stance, a bold stride, a dazzling jump. "There has to
be a bit of demon to start with," is one clause of his creed. No Man
o'War, no Secretariat ever came from a docile, intimidated colt.

So with Jesus; he went to the wilderness to wrestle not with a
Satan outside but with a demon within. A demon that fueled his
immense personal power and had to be tamed and disciplined and
directed. The wild beasts Mark mentions are Jesus' own: his stun-
ning personal attractiveness, his forceful physical presence, his
handsome, brilliant, manly, confident self—these are the beasts
that must be brought to bridle, trained to saddle and spur and
rein. This power must choose its goal and its destiny, its direction
and its purpose.

Even as must our own power. Great or small, each of us has been
given it and our task is to give it a reason and a justification, a
guiding value and an ultimate goal. Time and again we face these
choices in the extremities of life; however much they seem to be
wildernesses, we, like Jesus, are sent there by the Spirit.

---

*My uniqueness is your gift, my destiny is your service; school my
uniqueness, O God, in the requirements of my destiny.*

SATURDAY MORNING
READING: MARK 1:14–15

"After John had been arrested, Jesus came into Galilee proclaiming the Gospel of God: 'The time has come; the kingdom of God is upon you; repent, and believe the Gospel.'"

Much has been made by scholars of the competition between John and Jesus; there are evidences that after John's death his followers were reluctant to switch allegiances and never quite found a place for themselves in the circle around Jesus. The links between Jesus and John are something we don't know a great deal about and hence are surrounded by speculation and conjecture.

Notice the diffidence and respect with which Jesus treated John; he seemed to hold off the beginning of his own ministry, waiting for some kind of signal. He may have been waiting for a crucial difference to surface between them or for some indication of the completion of John's work of preparation. Mark takes the arrest of John to have been the signal Jesus needed; he announces Jesus' first public preaching with that event.

Jesus' first phrase declares the timeliness of his move into the public arena, and it is that element of timeliness I want to enlarge on. Each year I live deepens my belief in Providence, that mysterious work of God behind the changes and chances of life. "There's a divinity that shapes our ends, rough-hew them how we will," Hamlet says, in an admirable definition of God's action in shaping the course of a human life without violating human freedom.

A puzzling thing, a philosophical contradiction, a theological conundrum. But there it is: A timeliness, an appropriateness, a strange conspiracy of events, an unaccountable sequence that somehow leads us. "We know that in everything God works for good," Paul says. I believe it and so did Jesus: "The time has come."

Work the mystery of your Providence, Almighty Father, in the sequence of our lives; make us sensitive to your timing and responsive to your will.

SATURDAY EVENING
READING: MARK 1:15

"The Kingdom of God is upon you; repent, and believe the Gospel."

An interesting variety of translations has been made of the first part of Jesus' declaration: "the Kingdom of God is at hand," "has arrived," "is upon you," "is near," are just four. The Greek verb is in the perfect tense, expressing action that has been going on and is now complete; my preference is the New English Bible's "is upon you" because it conveys the sense of a completed pursuit: the Kingdom of God has caught up with you and is about to capture you at last.

Repentance and belief are the requirements to seal that capture. All the teaching and healing, the touching, the feeding, the words of comfort and challenge—all these things Mark subsequently records are Jesus' efforts to persuade us to believe: to believe the kingdom is near, upon us, about to catch up with us; to believe that God loves us, that he yearns for us, seeks us, that the Creation has groaned and labored to produce this moment and this encounter; to believe that the kingdom's door stands before us, open and welcoming, beckoning us to enter. All this to persuade us to believe, to trust; all this to help us repent.

For unless we believe, we can't repent; unless we trust, we can't surrender. There must be some reason, some hope, some promise, or we can't take on that revolution of values and behavior that repentance involves. The Gospel declaration is a simple statement, repent and believe; but the Gospel itself is never simplistic. Jesus' own patience and persistence in persuading us to believe demonstrates his grasp of the complexities involved and the repetitions required. No easy task is laid on us in those plain words: repent and believe. But the Gospel doesn't promise ease, it promises help.

I long for your kingdom, O God; help me believe your Gospel.

SUNDAY MORNING
READING: MARK 1:16

"Jesus was walking by the Sea of Galilee."

Mark's first personal word about Jesus finds him walking by the seashore, as countless of us have done—for the serenity, the majesty, the poetry of it. There is something irresistible about water; something in it calls to us, beckons us, and something very deep and primitive in us responds.

Water: so essential, so basic, so pervasive, so irreplaceable. I vividly remember learning that lettuce is 96 percent water (is it 94 percent? 98 percent? no matter, the point is the same) and going on to discover the incredible statistics of the percentage of water in all living tissue. And then I learned that we are nurtured in water; cradled and cushioned in an amniotic sea until we are born. So saturated with water is the whole physical world that it is the one thing the author of Genesis didn't have God create; it's just there: "And the Spirit of God moved up on the face of the waters." All God did was organize it: "Let there be a firmament in the midst of the waters, and let it divide the waters from the waters."

Again and again, Jesus is drawn to the Sea of Galilee; doubtless he saw the Mediterranean in his travels—Tyre and Sidon drew him to that coast—but his northern ministry centered on the shores of this lovely lake. Almost all people share with him the attraction of water—from the immensity of the ocean to the song of the splashing brook. He, too, experienced the mystery and the power of it, and when he needed a symbol of the ultimate cleansing for the sacrament of Baptism he reached, as had countless before him, to that most useful, most basic, most humble of God's gifts: water.

We delight in your Creation, Almighty God, in its beauty and its mystery, in the grand design of it all.

SUNDAY EVENING
READING: MARK 1:16–17

"Jesus was walking by the Sea of Galilee when he saw Simon and his brother Andrew on the lake at work with a casting-net; for they were fishermen. Jesus said to them, 'Come with me, and I will make you fishers of men.'

Jesus goes out to gather his band, and he begins with fishermen, Simon and his brother Andrew. The instructive thing about this is that Jesus began with what was at hand, he took for the stuff of his work the material God placed before him. I've spoken of Jesus' belief in Providence; this is another demonstration of it. He caught the signal of John's arrest and looked for his beginnings no further than his immediate surroundings. "Here is a community of fisher folk; God has summoned me to begin, he must mean for me to begin here." Something like that must have gone through his mind.

G. K. Chesterton has a marvelous essay about jury duty. In it he contrasts the role of the specialist, the educated, the professional, with the role of the common man. He observes that when society wants a new universe discovered, or "some such trifle as that," it calls in a highly educated, brilliant, and skilled professional, like an astronomer. But when it wants something really important decided, like the fate of a man accused of crime, it calls in twelve ordinary people, places them in a jury box and gives them this fateful power. "I seem to recall," Chesterton concludes, "that the Founder of Christianity did precisely the same thing."

He did, indeed; fishermen, ordinary people, people like you and me.

We give you what we are, O God; your power must make us what you want us to be.

Study Aids I

Perhaps you are familiar with the sermon illustration that helps us understand perspective. It involves a caterpillar who crawls slowly across an oriental rug, seeing only a random and meaningless sequence of colors. Having reached the border of the carpet, he becomes a butterfly and, taking wing, retraces his journey accross the rug. What was irregular and bewildering on his first trip has suddenly become an intricate and symmetrical pattern of beauty and craftsmanship.

Lest our trip through Mark resemble the caterpillar's first trip across the rug, we'll pause once a week to review what we have read and discuss or reflect on what we have learned. It might be useful to reread the week's material at one sitting, making notes on particularly helpful or particularly puzzling sections.

In these opening verses Mark is setting the stage for what is to follow, and we sense impatience on his part to get the introductory material out of the way. Those early verses are an enormous mine of information: an announcement of identity, the establishment of a connection with the Old Testament, a description of John the Baptist's activity, John's connection with Jesus, a promise of the Holy Spirit, a direct revelation to Jesus, a brief account of Jesus' sojourn in the wilderness, the arrest of John, Jesus' first public proclamation, the calling of the first disciples.

All of Mark is not that compact, but the events of Jesus' life as Mark recounts them would require only about six weeks to unfold. We are dealing with a highly selective record, a narrative that touches just the hilltops of our Lord's public life.

SUGGESTIONS FOR DISCUSSION AND REFLECTION:

Can you imagine this Gospel as your first information about Jesus? How would you respond to him?

Why would Jesus wait until the arrest of John to begin his public ministry?(1:14)

In preparing "a way for the Lord," what sorts of things get cleared from his path? (1:3)

Do you see any differences in the first proclamation of Jesus and the preaching of John the Baptist? John says nothing about faith or belief; is this significant?

From what Mark has said so far, would you picture Jesus and John as congenial? Competitive? Partners? Rivals?

How revolutionary a change is required by Jesus' command "Repent!"? (1:15) What has to be different?

Suppose Mark knew the stories of Jesus' birth recorded by Matthew and Luke; why would he omit them or any reference to them?

SECOND WEEK

MONDAY MORNING
READING: MARK 1:17–18

"Jesus said to them, 'Come with me, and I will make you fishers of men.' And at once they left their nets and followed him."

There's that little word "enthus," translated here as "at once." We will encounter it again where Mark wants to give a note of suddenness or urgency to his narrative. Here he employs it to convey the decisiveness with which Simon and Andrew responded to Jesus, the utter absence of hesitation in their obedience.

That's a marvelous picture; instant response, unflinching renunciation, unqualified commitment. I'm reminded of the writings of Dietrich Bonhoeffer, who speaks so movingly of obedience to Christ as a black-and-white thing: total, complete, unquestioning, unblemished. My problem is that that doesn't correspond to anything in my life. My vows of reform are fleeting, my faith is shadowed with uncertainties, my commitments evaporate like the puddles after a summer rain. My promises are eloquent, my performance is shabby; I adopt as my own Tallulah Bankhead's description of herself: "pure as the driven slush."

Where does that leave such a one as I? And maybe you? Where does that leave vacillating Peter? Ambitious John and James? Promiscuous Mary Magdalene? Thieving Zaccheus?

I take comfort in the fact that prophets deal in absolutes, read Isaiah or Jeremiah or Bonhoeffer. Pastors deal in ambiguities; read Jesus.

You summon us, Lord Jesus, just as you called Simon and Andrew; if our response is less complete, make your forgiveness no less generous.

MONDAY EVENING
READING: MARK 1:19-20

"When he had gone a little further he saw James son of Zebedee and his brother John, who were in the boat overhauling their nets. He called them; and, leaving their father Zebedee in the boat with the hired men, they went off to follow him."

James and John, another pair of brothers, respond as promptly as Simon and Andrew. One could get the feeling that something a little spooky is going on here, hypnosis of some kind, maybe. That isn't it at all. Jesus was acquainted here, he knew this area and these people. He may have been friends with these men, intimate even; they may have been waiting for him to come along some day and say, "Okay, time now to get started."

I'm certain Jesus had sized them up; just as I'm certain they had had the chance to listen to him. Remember the story he tells about seeds and soil, and the plants that sprang up quickly only to be choked out by "the cares and riches of this life"? Jesus is seeking no impulsive escapists, reforming the world one day and despairing of it the next. Remember the story he tells about building a tower, and how one must calculate the cost first? Same thing; he wants men who follow him with open eyes and with hearts that have wrestled over sacrifice and security, hearth and hardship.

And hearts that know the wrestling is never quite finished. That is, disciples prepared for the long pull and for the struggle within themselves, for the longings that plague any life of renunciation, for the doubts that haunt any life of commitment.

In short, disciples who depend not on their own powers, but, knowing Jesus, depend on his.

Keep us diligent in our discipleship, Master, and where we cannot be faithful, keep us humble, where we cannot be obedient, penitent.

TUESDAY MORNING
READING: MARK 1:21–22

"They came to Capernaum, and on the Sabbath he went to synagogue and began to teach. The people were astounded at his teaching, for, unlike the doctors of the law, he taught with a note of authority."

I believe there is only one authoritative teaching, and that is the teaching that arises out of experience. Authority is not attached to one's teaching by his vestments, his title, or his surroundings; authority comes from authenticity and authenticity comes from experience. Jesus had lived long enough and deeply enough to absorb the wisdom of his heritage, to test it in his own decisions and relationships and to give it the unique form and flavor of his own personal history. People recognize teaching like that.

Carl Jung makes an interesting observation about teaching: He says it takes place only when the teacher points out something the pupil already knows. That is, the teacher throws light on an insight the pupil is already struggling toward, has almost arrived at, has discovered without articulating. I have a friend who calls the best learning an "Aha!" experience, an experience that moves us to respond, "Yes, I knew that. I couldn't have put it in words, but that is just what I would have said if I could have."

All this points to the profoundly incarnational Jesus, a Jesus profoundly immersed in human flesh. He taught with authority because he'd seen through the struggle, unafraid of not knowing, unashamed of having to grope and grapple and go back again over the same ground until the light came. That's the human struggle for understanding and wisdom; Jesus shared it and that sharing gave him an authority his contemporaries recognized, an authority that is contemporary still.

Speak to the depths of our experience, Lord Jesus, and shed in that darkness the light of your wisdom.

TUESDAY EVENING
READING: MARK 1:21–28

"And the unclean spirit . . . left him."

A real puzzler; these obedient unclean spirits have always mys-
tified me. Why, if they recognize Jesus so easily and obey him so
readily, are they unclean spirits at all? Mark does add a note that
makes their obedience churlish and grudging: They seem always
to give their victims one last fit before they depart. But obedience
it is; Jesus says go and they go.

What can we say of an episode like this? Well, two things it
unquestionably teaches us: Knowledge that Jesus is the Son of God
doesn't save us; neither does snarling obedience to the letter of his
command.

The New Testament talks about spirit from start to finish and I
guess it is the spirit in which we recognize and obey that counts.
The motive, the intention, the feeling. If the spirit is unclean, it
seems to count little how accurate the recognition of the Son of
God or how precise the compliance to his command.

---

*You alone, Lord Jesus, know the mixture of sincerity and selfish-
ness in us; cleanse our motives and make them one.*

WEDNESDAY MORNING
READING MARK 1:29–34

"He healed many who suffered from various diseases."

Two accounts of healing follow in rapid succession after Jesus' first encounter with an unclean spirit; one is personal, one is public. Jesus managed to keep both facets of his ministry and his life—inseparable in him—in focus: he could reach and move his public, sometimes in the thousands, without forgetting the needs of those closest to him personally. A model for modern Christians, who have to balance large community duties—PTA, church, committees, breadwinning, politics, neighborhood, and the like—with the responsibilities of home and family, spouse and children. Like Jesus, we have demands both public and personal, in the home and out of it, and those demands require us to say no to some legitimate needs in order to say yes to other legitimate needs. No easy task, but a double pull that Jesus wrestled with every day.

This healing of Simon's mother-in-law involves the only mention of Peter's domestic life; his family appears nowhere else in the Gospel narrative. It makes us curious; we wonder if Peter didn't abandon his personal responsibilities for the demands of discipleship. We know a good deal about Peter; the New Testament follows him into the life of the early Church and reasonably authentic tradition follows him to a martyr's death in Rome. What of his wife and family all these years? What of the home to which he was so eager to bring Jesus? How well did Peter balance his public and his personal obligations? We can't answer; we only know he faced this struggle; and we must conclude that there is no single pattern for success, no single route to failure. There is only fidelity to the call of Christ; that fidelity insures the struggle and the mixture of success and failure we all experience and endure.

Help us in the struggle to balance conflicting responsibilities, O Lord, knowing this task belongs to our vocation as your disciples.

WEDNESDAY EVENING
READING: MARK 1:35–39

"He went away to a lonely spot and remained there in prayer."

That's a very appealing and serene picture: Jesus at prayer in the first hours of the day. Jesus, in that stillness, reflecting on yesterday's events, anticipating today's. That, in a sense, is all prayer: standing in the present moment, conscious of the present God; gathering every thought, every act, every relationship to his judgment; offering every choice, every opportunity, every possibility to his guidance. Offering repentance, claiming forgiveness; offering decision, claiming grace. This kind of transaction with God is meant to suffuse every moment; it establishes a beachhead in our preoccupations for the practice of conscious prayer, and conscious prayer begins with time set apart for it. Jesus needed that kind of time; so do we.

Jesus left the place of prayer reluctantly; so often our processes are just the reverse. We seek the place of prayer with dragging feet and leave it at the first provocation. Jesus left for the two reasons the story states so plainly: The crowds were seeking him, and his own inner imperative compelled him. They needed to hear; he needed to proclaim. These two components of any ministry met with such matchless harmony in him: their need for his gifts and his need to give. Such harmony is what every Christian seeks in serving God: that circumstance in which his urge to serve is matched by the need for his gifts.

The product of such a meeting of gift and need is that elusive thing we call happiness; the product of the search for such a meeting is that finer thing we call joy.

In returning and rest we shall be saved, in quietness and in confidence shall be our strength. Draw us to that returning, O God, and meet us in that quietness.

THURSDAY MORNING
READING: MARK 1:38–39

" 'I have to proclaim my message'. . . So all through Galilee he went, preaching in the synagogues and casting out the devils."

A marvelous statement for our time: timeless, and therefore peculiarly apt for this moment. Jesus sees his ministry as proclaiming, and Mark describes it as preaching and healing. To proclaim the Good News requires words and deeds, didaction and action, saying and doing. How can they be separate, and how can we argue whether both are necessary?

The church today is in a period of reflection, studying its record of intense involvement in social issues—an involvement that began in the early 1960s and has only lately tapered off. Being human, we find it difficult to concentrate on more than one thing at a time, and doubtless we need this time of respite to recapture some of the quieter things neglected in our decade-plus of activity. But life has changed and the church has changed and things will never be the same again.

That period of activity in the larger realms of our common life has left an indelible impress on the life of Christians: We will never worship again the way we did; we will never pray, never study Scriptures, never evaluate our pilgrimage the way we did before. Our understanding of what it means to answer the call of Christ in our time has been transformed: Once again we are in his footsteps, proclaiming the kingdom both ways, by the word of preaching and by the deed of casting out devils. By worship and prayer and study and learning, and by feeding and helping and healing and changing. Love is our message and it requires two languages: voice and action. Mark knew it long ago; how could we have forgotten?

Call us today, Lord Jesus, to the wholeness of your ministry, proclaiming the Good News by word and by deed.

THURSDAY EVENING
READING: MARK 1:40–45

"In warm indignation Jesus stretched out his hand."

Again, a healing. Here Mark takes time to notice Jesus' mood and labels it "warm indignation"; other translations use "compassion" or "pity." I like The New English Bible because it conveys the subtlety that there was something offensive to Jesus about sickness, something about any abnormality that affronted him. And this leads me to point out that his miracles always restored normality, put things to right, made things the way they were meant to be. Jumping off a pinnacle of the temple, that's showmanship, flaunting the abnormal; healing a leper, that's restoring the normal. Turning a stone into bread, that's blatant legerdemain; feeding the hungry, that's meeting a commonplace need.

But, for all this, Jesus bent over backwards to avoid the reputation of wonder worker and the role of "Mr. Fixit" that was certain to go with it. He wanted to do more than clean leprous bodies and banish epileptic demons; he sought to touch and command the heart, to revolutionize the goals and values and behavior. And so this curious insistence on secrecy, "Say nothing to anybody"; curious because he must have known how impossible a command he was issuing, how preposterous an expectation he was entertaining. Still the record is clear and frequent; time and again he commands silence and just as often he is disobeyed. I can see a wry smile cross his face as he watches the cured man run excitedly to spread the news, and, with a shrug of affectionate resignation, turns cheerfully to his next patient.

The gift of wholeness is in your hands, Lord Christ; heal us by the power of your touch.

FRIDAY MORNING
READING: MARK 2:1–12

"My son, your sins are forgiven."

Mark has recorded the astonishment that greeted Jesus' teaching. As the first content he will record, he chooses Jesus' teaching about forgiveness. Certainly our first need; and if not Jesus' first instruction then Mark's perception of our first urgency. These extraordinary friends dig up the adobe roof over Jesus' head and claim his attention by lowering the paralytic into his lap, as it were. Jesus spoke with affection and authority: "My son, your sins are forgiven." Notice Mark's insistence on the sequence: *"When* Jesus saw *their* faith, he said . . ." The friends' faith evoked Jesus' absolution; what are we to make of that?

There is in the world of philanthropy this thing called a multiplier. It operates in both public and private sectors and I'm never sure just which part of the formula is the multiplier and which is the multiplied. It works this way: You send a dollar to CARE and seven dollars worth of food arrives overseas. Government grants from surplus have multiplied your gift. Or a foundation gives fifty thousand dollars to an institution on the condition that it raise three dollars from others for every one dollar of its grant, and fifty is multiplied to two hundred. Or your eighty dollars given to the county is multiplied to one hundred and forty dollars worth of food stamps.

I think the same kind of thing operates with God's mercy: Neither my faith nor yours, my caring nor yours, can create it; but in some mysterious fashion we can multiply it, we can heighten it, focus it, precipitate it, evoke it. Love is like that, friendship is like that; yoked with God's power, it does astonishing things.

Add the immensity of your love, O God, to the modesty of ours, and multiply the power of our caring and our concern.

FRIDAY EVENING
READING: MARK 2:15–17

"I did not come to invite virtuous people, but sinners."

Again, by locating this exchange early in the Gospel, Mark affirms the centrality of forgiveness in Jesus' teaching. It's always tempting to compress the Gospel into one statement; preachers are notorious for it. Paul succumbed: ". . . Christ Jesus came into the world to save sinners," using two words, "save" and "sinners," that are in themselves ambiguous and inexact. Jesus is not quite so sweeping, but he does cut through layer upon layer of religious tradition and pride when he declares he is not in business for the virtuous but for the sinful.

The late Ted Wedel influenced a whole generation of American clergy; many of us remember vividly a story of his own crafting, which he loved to tell. It had to do with a lifesaving station that was built on a particularly hazardous rocky shore. At first a group of shore dwellers caulked up an old boat and beached it near the site of shipwrecks, where it would be readily available for emergency use. Canon Wedel elaborated the narrative with relish; I'll give you just the outline: Then came a launchway for the boat, then a shed; then a room for training and meetings; then an auxiliary to raise money for curtains; then bake sales and rummage sales and carpeting on the floor. Then the construction of a "liturgical" boat which didn't really move and had cushioned seats and dummy oars for "liturgical" excercises; then officers and a treasurer and a building-and-grounds committee, a ways-and-means committee, a membership committee, and way down on the chart an operations committee, which was hard to get a chairman for and nobody wanted to serve on anyway. You get the point. The shipwrecks were forgotten and the life-saving station became a playground for people who had no sense of danger or need, and avoided involvement with anyone who did.

Churches get this way, and the sickly, the failed, the overwhelmed-by-life, are never considered by the membership committee. Jesus is among those who don't apply.

Keep before us, Lord Jesus, the lonely, the forgotten, the powerless of the world, and remind us it is for them you came and to them we are sent.

SATURDAY MORNING
READING: MARK 2:23–28

"The Sabbath was made for the sake of man."

Two episodes on forgiveness, and now revolution. I struggle to articulate the enormity of these twelve simple words. "The Sabbath was made for man and not man for the Sabbath." Jesus overturns in one sweeping statement the abusive authority organized religion is so tempted to arrogate to itself. Jesus claims that the good of man—his growth, his development, his fulfillment, his happiness—is the reason for religion, and hence religion is man's servant and not his master.

Religion is a peculiar and much misused word. It derives from a Latin root that means "bind up," "pull together," "give cohesion to." Religion is meant to make sense of life, to give it flavor and purpose and hope and delight. It is meant to affirm life's variety and to celebrate its diversity. It is meant to guide life, to correct it, to assist it, to nurture it. Religion is not meant to substitute for life; it is not meant to confine life and discourage it; not meant to conventionalize and standardize it; not meant to reduce life to rules and regulations and proscriptions and inhibitions. Religion is not mankind's tormenter and common scold, it is his wisdom and his endurance and his light.

In *Travels with Charlie*, John Steinbeck reported he found the food served along America's highways uniformly packaged, uniformly sanitary, and uniformly tasteless. When men and women become the servants of religion instead of the other way around, the same thing happens to people. As Pete Seeger would say, "We all come out in little boxes and we all look just the same." We were not made for religion; religion is made for us.

Make our religion as large as your Creation, O God, and keep near its center your promise of abundant life.

SATURDAY EVENING
READING: MARK 3:1–6

"Is it permitted to do good or to do evil on the Sabbath?"

Once again the Sabbath regulations rear their suffocating disapproval and once again Jesus rebels. Mark notes Jesus' emotions: "... anger and sorrow at their obstinate stupidity." How often that stupidity was to plague him, in both enemies and friends. But the enemies are not so stupid that they fail to recognize Jesus for who he is: a dangerous and inflammatory revolutionary.

Politics produces strange bedfellows; religious politics too. Here two natural enemies—Pharisee and Herodian—make common cause against Jesus. From the beginning he has been the enemy of entrenched power; he will be until the bloody end. An unholy alliance of church and state is represented here: the Herodians of royal prerogative, the Pharisees of religious status. There is no record that they remembered, but that royal party had plotted once before against the life of Jesus; the soldiers of an earlier generation may have forgotton about the babe of Bethlehem, thinking him disposed of in the slaughter some thirty years before.

The shadow of this bitter resistance to Jesus will cloud the rest of the Gospel story; eager response to an ennobling message is so often all that is portrayed of the early Galilean ministry. But the darker side is there, a deep and silent current that will gather force and finally burst shatteringly to the surface. And that current is in each of us, that resistance is not foreign to us; there is in every Christian that prized indulgence, that protected sin, that secret disobedience that senses threat in Jesus and would silence him if it could.

In every response of ours, Lord Jesus, there is reluctance; in every surrender, resistance; in every request there is reservation, save in this one plea: forgive.

SUNDAY MORNING
READING: MARK 3:13–19

"He appointed twelve as his companions."

Humanity was created social and every one of us involves three people: self, father, and mother. The tensions associated with that triangle stay with us, and in every relationship this question applies: How can I be myself, and being myself still be a member of the community? The fulfillment of the human creation lies in that ultimate community in which each of us is honored and loved for who he is, and in which each of us honors and loves every other for his identity, his gifts, and his limitations. So Jesus forms a community, called out of their diversity—Peter impulsive, James and John bombastic, Thomas skeptical, Simon zealous, Judas cunning—to form a company of common work, common values, and common mutual respect.

That company takes some building, and Mark makes no attempt to disguise the problems. There is shallowness, rivalry, reluctance, doubt, betrayal—all the frailties of discipleship we encounter in church today. There was no instant paradise then, any more than there is now; the fashioning of a responsive, obedient community is a process that is never complete. The Book of Acts records the tumultuous life of the first-generation church and the epistles are addressed to its difficulties; hence the New Testament is not a description of heaven, it's a manual for building and maintaining community in Christ.

An early Christian apologist proclaims: For the church the world was made. He means not the institution—top-heavy, self-aggrandizing, timid and vacillating—but that community in which all people find themselves needed and esteemed. That is the ideal toward which the real struggles; Jesus believes the ideal has no meaning if it is not clothed in flesh and blood, and so he gathers these twelve and begins with them.

––––––––––––––––

Call us again to your companionship, O Lord; we long for your leadership and hunger for your heroism.

SUNDAY EVENING
READING: MARK 3:20–21, 31–35

"They set out to take charge of him."

Why is it that those who mean best by us are so often those who do us worst? Why is it that those closest to us are so often the last to understand us? I suppose doubts about the sanity of this carpenter's son were bound to arise sooner or later; interesting that they took root so quickly in his immediate family. The New English Bible's language is wonderfully graphic: "they set out to take charge of him." I can see them: bewildered mother, troubled sisters, disapproving and jealous brothers.

Jesus handles the situation masterfully; his resolution is a measure of his maturity as a person and his confidence in his calling. You remember the old bromide: "They called him heretic, thing to flout, and drew a circle that shut him out; but love and I were determined to win, we drew a circle that took him in." Jesus might have winced at the poetry, but it describes quite accurately what he did. He renounced his family's claim on him, their suspicion of his sanity and their over-protective concern, but he did it without rancor or harshness or scorn. He simply drew for his family a larger circle that included countless more without excluding them. Instead of rejecting them or replacing them, he simply swept them into a definition of family that they shared with others; he took nothing from them in giving their special place to anyone who chose to accept it.

Isn't this the way love always works? Always reaching for a larger circle, a wider embrace?

Teach us again, dear Jesus, this miracle of love: That it is more blessed to give than to receive, that it is in giving we gain.

Study Aids II

This week's reading has taken Jesus here and there in Galilee, from lakeside to village street, encountering both success and opposition. These opposite responses begin to coalesce in the narrative covered, people begin to choose sides. On the one side, Jesus selects from among those who have responded positively to him "the men he wanted." On the other side, "the Pharisees begin plotting against him with the partisans of Herod."

Jesus attaches nicknames to the first three apostles named: "Rocky" for Simon, "Hotheads" for the sons of Zebedee (literally, sons of thunder). These informalities betray an easy comradeship among these thirteen men on the threshold of an adventure that will overturn the world; that mood matches the pastoral environment of the lush hills of Galilee and the spirit of optimism and expectation in which this "movement" began.

Mark calls particular attention to Jesus in the synagogue, and to his Sabbath behavior; it might be worth counting the references to that specific building and that day of the week. Healing and teaching occupy about equal space in Mark's account, and the section ends with the ill-fated visit of reclamation by Jesus' family.

SUGGESTIONS FOR DISCUSSION AND REFLECTION:

Why did Jesus forbid spirits and healed persons to identify him?

How would you explain that Jesus forgives the paralytic's sin on the basis of his friends' faith? (2:5)

Has it ever occurred to you that Jesus' behavior was provocative? (2:15, 2:23, 3:2)

When Jesus makes the Sabbath the servant of man, what becomes of religious authority? (2:27–28)

What made the Pharisees angry? Were they overreacting? (3:6)

Does the visit of Jesus' family (3:20ff) remind you of parents of Moonies, followers of Sun Myung Moon? What is the difference?

Can you identify yourself with either side of the story—misunderstood offspring or concerned parent?

Five controversy stories follow in quick succession. (2:6–3:6) Does the preaching of the Gospel then and now inevitably provoke conflict?

The easiest outline of Mark is a geographical one; it might be instructive to go back over his place names with a good Bible atlas and fix in your mind the sequence of Jesus' travels.

THIRD WEEK

MONDAY MORNING
READING: MARK 3:22–30

"Whoever slanders the Holy Spirit can never be forgiven."

There is a marvelous exchange in one of the Gilbert and Sullivan operettas, in which one character declares with firmness and finality, "Never!" Another responds with skepticism, "Never?" and the first replies, "Well, hardly ever."

"Never" is a very large word, and I recall that modification of it in connection with this declaration of Jesus, "Whoever slanders the Holy Spirit can never be forgiven." I hope not. I hope Jesus means something different from what that says on the surface. It seems so unlike him to close doors and nail them shut for eternity, so out of character with the rest of what we know about him. I agree with Halford Luccock who says he'd list this statement under the heading, "Things I wish Jesus had never said."

My only consolation is to look at it from the side of the Holy Spirit. I just can't imagine the Holy Spirit "feeling slandered," pouting, nursing a wound, indulging pique, plotting revenge. From our side, saying and doing slanderous things is all too likely; from God's side, finding words so offensive to him, so heinous and extreme as to warrant the judgment "unforgivable!" seems just plain inconceivable. That reduces God to an insecure and easily affronted minor deity.

Do you remember the old childhood taunt: "Sticks and stones can break my bones but words can never hurt me?" We took sticks and stones to the Son of God and literally killed him, and we stand forgiven; surely our rash and hasty words are forgivable too.

Bend your every compassion to our need, loving Father, and meet our most hateful sin with your most generous forgiveness.

MONDAY EVENING
READING: MARK 4:1–20

"And he taught them many things by parables."

Again, Jesus by the lakeside, drawn, like his hearers, by the mystery, the beauty, the solace of water. I caught my first view of the Sea of Galilee as we topped the hill above the city of Tiberias; it lay before us, sparkling in the March sun, charged with history and memory and promise. Shells landed in Tiberias that day in 1962, a sobering reminder that the Prince of Peace who walked these shores is unheeded still.

In the middle of the story of sower and seed there stands another of my candidates for the list of things I wish he hadn't said. What can we make of Jesus' statement that he tells the truth with deliberate obscurity so that some will "hear but understand nothing; otherwise they might turn to God and be forgiven"? Heavens! What's it all for if it isn't to encourage people to turn to God, to enable them to be forgiven? It flies in the face of what we believe of him to suppose that he'd create a little "in group," with its own lingo, so that "outsiders" wouldn't catch on and get saved.

I raised this question in a seminary class and got a masterfully obscure reply: "It has to do with the breakdown of tense in the Hebrew verb." Well, if my salvation goes down the drain because the Hebrew verb has problems with tense, then my conviction that grammar is the invention of the devil is simply confirmed.

If Jesus said what these words mean, there is an explanation that has so far escaped us; until that explanation is revealed, I'm going to believe he said something else.

Come to us in the pages of the Gospel, good Jesus, and when we falter in the light of your truth, we will rejoice in the light of your presence.

TUESDAY MORNING
READING: MARK 4:21–23

"If you have ears to hear, then hear."

This I can buy: Jesus has not obscured his truth or hidden his lamp, but he leaves it to us whether or not we will respond. This is the marvelous mystery of human freedom, a powerful and a puzzling thing. Jesus does not coerce or manipulate; he wins us in our freedom, through our freedom, not around our freedom or at the cost of our freedom.

God made us to choose and he loves us into choosing him. Blind obedience he has plenty of—the whole creation sings a song of obedience. The birds fly south on signal; the squirrels bury nuts on command; the whole natural cycle turns in response to God's will. The splendid household of nature maintains, in obedience to his providence, a wonderful balance of life; a grand evolution of species and habitat; a march of development, adaptation, and mutation; a great and complex symphony of life; a sacred sequence of creation—plastic and responsive in God's hands.

But men and women are free, created to choose; not given unlimited choice, but choice enough to decide our fate, to accept or reject our destiny, to claim or renounce our fulfillment. We've wrestled from the beginning with the philosophical puzzle of negative choice—sin, error, stupidity, stubbornness, rejection—of evil in a good world, designed and created good by a good God. Its explanation is as elusive as its fact is unavoidable. We are free; we can choose disobedience, rebellion, refusal.

Jesus respects that freedom; if you have ears to hear, then hear.

We mean to hear, we mean to understand, we mean to obey; heal, O Christ, our deafness, our stupidity, and our rebellion.

TUESDAY EVENING
READING: MARK 4:24–25

"The measure you give is the measure you will receive."

It seems unfair, doesn't it? It sounds like the cynicism of the lame old joke: "the rich get richer and the poor get children." Jesus says two things: One speaks of giving, one speaks of having. Let's look at the one that talks about giving: "The measure you give is the measure you will receive, with something more besides."

Jesus is describing the way things are, and it's an observation any of us could make. I encountered a story in my childhood called "How Cedric Became a Knight." It was set in medieval England and recounted the long training and trial process that led Cedric from serfdom to knighthood. I read it again and again. There were no shortcuts, no quickie curricula. There were long years, hard work, hard study, hard testing. Cedric gave his best; life gave him its best in return.

Life cares about such things and is thoroughly moral in its response to us. Life forgives and forgives again, but it does not reward sloth, nor does it treat dedication and indifference alike. Two friends spend an afternoon on a wooded path; one counts forty-seven species of birds, the other remembers seeing only three birds altogether, none identifiable. What's the difference? One has given attention, concentration, interest, study; the other has given nothing. The measure you give is the measure you get. A hard saying? No, a simple reality.

Effort, discipline, tenacity—listen, it makes a difference if you give these things; life responds to you in a different way. If you want to be lazy and careless, life will love you and life will forgive you. But make no mistake, life will be different.

Hold before us the truths of life, Lord Jesus, and teach us that as there is forgiveness for every mistake, so there is consequence to every decision.

WEDNESDAY MORNING
READING: MARK 4:26–34

"The seed sprouts and grows—how, he does not know."

I used to enjoy doing a stunt in church-school sermon time. I'd display a flowerpot of dirt and ask the youngsters how they could eat that dirt. We would wrestle with that impossibility with varying degrees of success, depending on the answers my questions evoked. Then I'd show them a flowerpot with a carrot growing in it. I would explain that to get at the nutrition in the soil, it had to be transformed into a carrot or a potato or something we could eat, and that the way this happened was utterly mysterious to us and utterly beyond our powers to duplicate. I'd emphasize that in all the world there is only one process that makes food—sunlight on a green plant—and that how it works remains shrouded in mystery.

Jesus applies that mystery to the kingdom of God; from the first planting of the seed in our hearts to the full maturity of our sonship, the kingdom grows, we know not how. We know many things we can do that help or hinder, many ways we can affect its development, but the how of it belongs to the mystery of God's love, his patient, caring, tireless yearning for us. There is mystery in its planting, in our cooperative role, in the whole matter of size—from tiny seed to stately tree. Jesus says the growth of the reign of God in our lives is like that.

While he would be the last to counsel indifference, he does counsel trust. The farmer in the story lives his daily round—"he goes to bed at night and gets up in the morning"—and lo the seed grows and prospers and the harvest comes.

Keep us aware, O Lord, of the mystery of the most commonplace, and in each mystery help us to see your hand, your presence, your love.

WEDNESDAY EVENING
READING: MARK 4:35–41

"He rebuked the wind and said to the sea, 'Hush! Be still!' "

The wind and the sea obey him. All right, they were dumbfounded and so are we; it struck them as strange and alarming—little wonder it strikes us that way too. This episode opens a section of Mark that The New English Bible entitles "Miracles of Christ." A word about miracles in general may be in order.

I've said already that Jesus' miracles are directed toward restoration of the normal, the expected—not at the creation of the spectacular or the bizarre. It is true here. We cannot believe these experienced fishermen had not long since learned the canons of safety in stormy waters. This storm must have been extraordinary in its suddenness or its violence and called forth from Jesus the same concern as sickness or crippled limbs. "Dead calm" may be Mark's exaggeration; at any rate Jesus' command reduced the storm to manageable proportions.

There is something operating here that we don't understand and therefore it strains our credibility. Teilhard has taught us that the creation moves from the most rudimentary of inanimate material to the immense complexity of the human person in one straight, uninterrupted line. One corollary of this is that there is a kind of kinship between the human spirit and inanimate material that we haven't yet perceived or explored. We've noted the kinship with water—why not wind and rocks? Wasn't the psalmist feeling something of this kinship when he cried, "I will lift up mine eyes unto the hills"? Plants prosper when people talk to them. I take that at face value. Why not?

So Jesus speaks, and the wind and sea obey; a miracle, yes. But, as before, moving away from the unusual and the ominous toward the manageable, the reassuring, the normal.

We ask no miracles of showmanship or sensation, Lord Christ, but only those gifts that measure our need of you: trust, calm, courage.

THURSDAY MORNING
READING: MARK 5:1–20

"My name is Legion."

This is one of the longer narratives in Mark, and we wonder why he singles it out for such detailed treatment. Jesus is in a non-Jewish part of the country; he has a most baffling conversation with an unclean spirit; the episode created great public excitement. It seems to be the lone event of this visit to the Gerasene shore.

The unclean spirit names himself "Legion," and for once we discover ourselves touched and moved by these strange creatures. There is in that name such a heavy hopelessness, in the weariness of that plea such a vast and oppressive burden; it's as if, having abandoned bravado and defiance, the demon's mask falls away and the pitiable, ravaged face of evil is revealed. It must have caught Jesus off guard and tugged at his heartstrings; so he gave the spirits leave to go where they would, and the pigs were destroyed. A thousand loose ends are left dangling.

At the end, the healed man begs to go with Jesus, but he is told, "Go home to your own folk." This from the native son who observed that a prophet is honored everywhere except in his own country. Provost Williams of Coventry recites a fine poem about a seaman who is converted and dreams of the people he will preach to when he quits the sea. But in the dream Jesus commands him to stay where he is and preach to those he knows and whose lot he has shared.

So with the Gerasene demoniac; he is sent healed and transformed to those who knew him as fierce and wild, to make, from his own history, his own irreplaceable witness to the power of God.

———————————

Cast out our demons, O Christ, and send us to confess your name by the power of lives made whole and joyous.

THURSDAY EVENING
READING: MARK 5:17

"They begged Jesus to leave the district."

A comment about this terse request. After all, two thousand pigs is no small investment, and so what if Jews don't eat pork, do they have any right to go around killing pigs? Who is this fellow, anyway? and where does he get off coming over here and mucking things up?

A natural enough response; two thousand pigs is quite an operation, and the swineherds were simply going about their innocent business. It isn't Jesus' last interference with commerce: the moneychangers of the temple felt his direct wrath, and Paul found himself invited out of town by irate silversmiths who discovered his preaching against idols was not good for business.

We have to recognize that the kingdom is costly in all the ways we can anticipate and in some we cannot. Its coming leaves nothing unchanged; it overturns all our values and is bound to disrupt many of our otherwise innocent patterns and habits. We must be prepared to hold nothing back from the transforming power of Christ in us, to shield nothing from his judgment and his conversion.

Swineherds and silversmiths may have to turn to other things; remember, he lays nothing on us he doesn't share, he makes no requirement without making the way.

Claim the whole of us, Lord Christ, body and soul, and free us from the tyranny of those things we would withhold from you.

FRIDAY MORNING
READING: MARK 5:25–34

"If I touch even his clothes, I shall be cured."

This story belies the title The New English Bible editors gave this section, "Miracles of Christ." By Jesus' own word to the woman who found healing, it was her miracle and not his: "Your faith has cured you." The place of faith in healing looms large in our awareness, even if we haven't quite codified or systematized it yet. I am constantly surprised by reports of the power of inert placebos to work healing very like potent drugs do; apparently, the patient's confidence in the healing power of an innocuous pill is sufficient to effect a cure.

This woman brought immense faith to her contact with Jesus, and an optimism that kept her seeking a cure. She trusted that if she could just connect with the edge of his presence healing would come, and so it did. Stammering with embarrassment and disbelief, she confessed her "theft" to Jesus, only to have what she had gained by stealth given by love.

Jesus felt power go out of him, and that's been helpful for me to know. Years ago my seminary dean, Henry Shires, applied that small description of Jesus' experience to the pastoral ministry; he said it confirms that helping people is hard work and that it's legitimate to feel drained at the end of the day. If so powerful and resourceful a helper as Jesus felt the subtraction of energy at this light touch, it's all right for you and me to feel weariness when we have given of ourselves. He knew where to go for restoration and so do we.

We come to you as to a fountain of living water, Lord Jesus; wash away our weariness and restore our energies.

FRIDAY EVENING
READING: MARK 6:1–6

"And they fell foul of him."

The power of a closed mind. The hometown phenomenon. Jesus helpless before human freedom. And, once again, the role of faith in healing.

It is striking how quickly the unbelieving spirit seizes upon contempt as a weapon of defense. Very early in my ministry I was given a timely and helpful warning. I've forgotten what I had said in my sermon, but after church a caring person said, "I don't believe we ever make points by talking down someone else's religion." I was acutely embarrassed but the lesson stuck. Since then I've responded, as my parishioner did, with pain and chagrin, when I've heard someone belittle another's faith. It is a weapon of weakness and the defense of a small mind. Let another's faith or practice stand on its own; it doesn't have to make sense to us to be helpful to him, and we only betray our own uncertainty when we resort to ridicule.

How Jesus must have wanted to serve these neighbors and kinsmen; but he seems not to have tarried over his defeat. Other voices called to him, other hearts awaited him—so he went on, not looking back, but carrying with him one small corner of regret. Nobody likes failure, nobody who loved so intensely and so uncritically as Jesus. But human freedom can erect an impenetrable barrier; it is the nature of love to respect it.

Help us honor every seeking person, dear Lord, and to respect the right of every soul to choose its own response to your ministry and to ours.

SATURDAY MORNING
READING: MARK 6:14–29

"Herod liked to listen to him, although the listening left him greatly perplexed."

"Ah, yes," he said, cradling his chin in his hand, "yes, yes. Complex, yes, complex; very perplexing, yes, quite perplexing. Hmm." I can just see King Herod responding to John the Baptist, a figure who fascinated and frightened him at one and the same time. He couldn't obey him, yet he couldn't turn loose of him; this reckless prophet both offended him and attracted him. Very perplexing, yes, quite perplexing.

I love that: "Herod went in awe of John . . . he liked to listen to him, although the listening left him greatly perplexed." Perplexed my eye; he knew exactly what John meant and it scared him to death. Perplexity is the first available shelter for someone who has just seen the light, just heard the word, just finally grasped what's really involved. Better think this over, better give this some time, better back off here. "Ah, yes, very interesting, interesting indeed. Yes. Oh complex, very complex. Yes, deep; deep and perplexing, yes, quite perplexing." Hogwash. That's not a reflective and searching response; that's backing water and getting out as fast as possible.

We recognize it because we've done it too; we've sought the shelter of perplexity when the Gospel demands too much, when its total claim comes home to us with renewed force. You and I and old Herod are not so different: scratch a perplexed listener and you find a scared disciple.

There are ambiguities, my faith is incomplete, I don't really surrender everything; Jesus wants that confession. Better we should turn away like the rich young ruler, because we have so much to lose, than to keep Jesus in the custody of our indecision. He will be back.

Help us to gaze without shrinking on the cross of your sacrifice, dear Lord, and to answer your call without bravado or pretense.

SATURDAY EVENING
READING: MARK 6:30–44

"They all ate to their hearts' content."

The early church, in its eucharistic devotion and symbolism, re-called much more frequently than we this feeding by the lakeside. Our liturgies and our ornamentation connect Holy Communion almost exclusively with the Last Supper, and this, in a very subtle way, has robbed our eucharistic services of some of the festive, celebrative spirit they ought to have. After all, what we have here is a gigantic picnic. The setting is ideal, the food is plentiful, the whole thing is well organized. "They all ate to their hearts' content." A great success, a delightful occasion; it had everything but sack races and an egg toss.

On the other hand, our liturgy, recalling exclusively the Last Supper as antecedent, is sober with betrayal and crucifixion, heavy with penitence and guilt. Try as we will to cheer the eucharist with triumphal music and the color and motion of celebration, the core of it always brings us back to the sequence of Holy Week and walks us through the dark streets of that memory.

Of course, we can't forget it, we can't undo it. But it's all bathed in Resurrection light now; Easter has happened, the strife is over, the victory is won. Can't we journey to this happy hillside once in a while? Can't we recall a meal that surprised hungry people and brought smiles to their faces and contentment to their bellies and maybe cheers to their lips?

It occurs to me the picnic was a more eucharistic occasion than Maundy Thursday. We remember Holy Week every year, must we relive betrayal and arrest and crucifixion every week? The good news is Easter; let's open up the liturgy and let it in.

Recall us to that happy hillside, dear Savior; relax and cheer us with the food of your presence.

SUNDAY MORNING
READING: MARK 6:45–52

"Take heart! It is I; do not be afraid."

In *Jesus Christ Superstar*, Pontius Pilate sings a mocking song in which he taunts Jesus to "walk across my swimmin' pool." It draws a big laugh. I suppose there is no other episode over which clergy are victimized by more tiresome humor and thinly disguised ridicule than this of Jesus walking on water. I confess it is a confusing narrative to me. Anyone who has walked along the margins of the sea knows water is no pleasure to trudge through; if Jesus had powers of "levitation" it would have been much simpler just to overleap the lake. It seems like a flaunting of pointless powers, especially since Jesus apparently had no intention of catching up with his friends or even of passing close enough to be visible. Mark seems to include himself in the phrase "they were completely dumbfounded"; I count myself in that astonished company too. I'm baffled.

Except for one thing: it is better when he is with us. Any fear, any anxiety or dread or apprehension eases in his presence; the winds of terror abate when we sense he is aboard. There is this awful thing about being alone, about facing some stark reality without another's presence. Time and again in the pastoral ministry I have realized that the presence of the minister is what makes the difference; not what he says, but who he is and, more to the point, whom he brings.

That part of the story is crystal clear; however he reaches us, once he's there things improve.

Find us in the moments of our need, Lord Jesus, whatever the setting or the means of your coming.

SUNDAY EVENING
READING: MARK 6:53–56

"Wherever he went, they laid out the sick."

There was no escape for Jesus; he sought solitude but there was nowhere he was not recognized and mobbed. Of course, as he said earlier, "This is what I came out to do." Still, there is a point of diminishing returns when effectiveness is blunted by boredom if not plain physical exhaustion. There seemed to be no slowing down for him.

The New English Bible titles the next section "Growing Tension," and while most of that is precipitated by Jesus' opponents, unquestionably some of it comes from within him. Patience is shortened by fatigue, concentration is dulled, facial muscles tighten, gait and posture betray distraction. Not good for one who wants to focus attention and energy on each pleading spirit; and so tension rises within Jesus as he struggles for poise and command.

We are tempted to think of the Galilean ministry as bucolic, successful, fulfilling, and of the Jerusalem ministry as soured by hostility and conflict. We overlook the unrelenting pressure of crowds and the steady drain on energies, which must have blurred Jesus' sense of satisfaction in the glad response he met. Already there's an undertone of flight and the sense that there is no turning back.

Another Gospel records Jesus saying, "He who lays his hand to the plow and looks back is not worthy of the Kingdom of God." The statement must have been forming in his mind about this time, when he shakes off his weariness, sets his shoulders, and strides into a darkening future.

Our hope takes new life from your endurance, Lord Jesus; renew our flagging spirits by your sturdy grace.

Study Aids III

Mark's geography divides Jesus' public life broadly into three sections: Galilean (the first six and a half chapters), wider journeys (the end of chapter 6 through chapter 9), and Jerusalem (chapters 10 through 16). The narrative read in our third week sees the end of the strictly Galilean ministry of Jesus and the beginning of wider travel. Not too much can be made of this because Mark's geographical and historical details are often inaccurate, but this general outline of Jesus' ministry was adopted by the other Gospel writers, through John makes important departures.

The sequence seems logical enough; at least it violates no historical necessity we can discern and no scholar's improvement has ever gained wide acceptance. We need to modify this only by the observation that Mark's chronology is doubtless too brief; John's three-year period is universally accepted as more accurate.

We can count sixteen episodes and discourses in the reading this week; historical material dominates with parables, healings, and miracles in roughly equal numbers. Mark gives much space to the parable of the sower and its explanation, to the demoniac who named himself Legion, and to the story of John the Baptist's death.

Mark forces no thematic scheme on his material but spreads it somewhat randomly across the geographical outline. The earliest logical sequences of events and teachings begin to emerge only after the shadow of impending death falls across the narrative.

SUGGESTIONS FOR DISCUSSION AND REFLECTION:

About the parable of the sower, 4:1–20:
> What kind of soil am I? How could I improve?
> What kind of soil is my church? How could we improve that?
> What are some of the weeds that choke the seed today?
> Why is the sower so careless with the seed?
Is the Kingdom of God of this world or the next?
> Is it obvious or hidden? Is it built by God or by men and women? (4:1–34)
Why did the demoniac run toward Jesus instead of away from him? (5:6)
Have you ever wished Jesus would leave you alone? (5:17)
How would you describe what Jesus has done for you? (5:20)
Does the reply of the disciples seem testy to you? (5:31)
What do we make of serious prayer for healing that doesn't work?
Have you known illustrations of Jesus' observation about prophets in their own country? (6:4) Exceptions?
Early Christians closely associated the Holy Communion with the feeding of the multitudes. (6:35–44) Do you see connections?
What did Jesus mean by the "secret of the Kingdom of God?" (4:11; see also 4:26, 30)

FOURTH WEEK

MONDAY MORNING
READING: MARK 7:1–8

"Why do your disciples not conform?"

On stage strides the enemy, cloaked in the power of the establishment, reeking of rectitude and respectability, secure in position and prestige. And what does he discover? Why, shame of shame and scandal of scandal, this bumpkin eats without washing his hands! I hope it made Jesus laugh; all the way from Jerusalem to indict him for this. They've missed the whole point, they haven't heard a thing, and they go their merry way teaching as doctrines the commandments of men.

It needs to be said that they had a good idea in that washing-hands business; it would be long centuries before the germ theory of disease made that practice a commonplace and vindicated this ancient wisdom. Curious how many things ancient man knew of agriculture, nutrition, public health, and the like without a clue as to the reason.

But to make a ritual practice into a moral issue, that is a grave mistake, and to build a case against Jesus on such flimsy grounds is sheer folly. We do less of this now than we used to. There was a day when ceremonial niceties led to stormy disputes in the church; we are occupied now with weightier matters.

Jesus understood that this picking at the edges of his proclamation would never be more than a nagging nuisance, but his sense of urgency lowered the threshold of his tolerance of these ecclesiastical gnats, and it all just tightened the screws of tension under which he labored and from which there was no escape.

Remind us daily, dear Lord, of your single command of love, and help us keep secondary things in second place.

MONDAY EVENING
READING: MARK 7:14–23

"It is what comes out of a man that defiles him."

What patent wisdom, what splendid insight. How, indeed, can anything from without defile me? Defilement comes from within, from the heart, where all those dismal things on Jesus' list have their origin. I once heard a preacher say, "I never saw a divided congregation that wasn't an inside job." He meant the same thing; whatever outside circumstances may have occasioned the division, the congregation itself let it happen, let it divide them, let anger and pettiness and strife take over.

In the middle of the paragraph, Mark inserts a word of interpretation: "Thus he declared all foods clean." It may be a gloss on the margin of an early copy that has found its way into the text. It has far-reaching application: Peter struggled with his own strict conscience even after a vision had reinforced Jesus' words; Paul struggles with it in the young churches that bring Jew and Gentile to a common table; we struggle with it in reference to alcohol. Making all foods clean may raise more problems than it settles, but then it is the nature of Gospel freedom to be subject to the abuse of license; Paul spends some of his most labyrinthine eloquence on that issue.

A word about our practice of grace before meals: The Jews blessed God, not the food, in thanksgiving for the nourishment and the pleasure of his gifts. I wish we would do that. It is a joyous thing to gather at table, the food is the blessing, the company is the delight, the whole experience is a wonderful wedding of the pleasures of body and spirit. Blessed be God indeed, and blessed be his Kingdom.

We bless you, O God, for all your gracious gifts: food, shelter, work, leisure; the pleasures of life and the promise of eternity.

TUESDAY MORNING
READING: MARK 7:24–30

"He would have liked to remain unrecognized, but this was impossible."

Again, the futile withdrawal from the crowd's demands. But how costly this retreat would have been had it succeeded. For God had an important lesson to teach his son in this encounter, a watershed lesson for him and for us.

In this reluctant exchange with this Gentile woman, Jesus learns a new dimension of his ministry. In an expanded version of this conversation in another Gospel, Jesus declares, "I am not sent but to the lost sheep of the house of Israel." He goes on with an almost brutal chauvinism to compare his healing her daughter with robbing a child's food to feed a dog. I must say this determined woman did not flinch at that harsh rejection, but came back with a rejoinder that showed spirit and wit and opened Jesus' eyes to a new perspective of himself and of his ministry to all people, Jew and Gentile unlike.

So does Providence push us into situations we can grow on, situations we would avoid if we could, maybe just because we sense they will make new demands on us, demands we are not prepared to meet or perhaps even acknowledge.

So does God proclaim our maturity never complete, our pilgrimage never ended, our need for learning and growth and wisdom never satisfied. Jesus was learning still; so are we.

Help us, O Lord, to learn from every encounter; to deal with every person as with a teacher, and to grow in each relationship.

TUESDAY EVENING
READING: MARK 7:31–37

"He even makes the deaf hear and the dumb speak."

Jesus went promptly on into Gentile territory and without hesitation answered a Gentile plea for help. Mark nails the whole transformation down by preserving the very Greek word Jesus used in the healing. His ministry is now universal; his vision embraces all men and women.

I relish the response of the crowd to Jesus' miracle: "He makes the deaf hear and the dumb speak." He does so still, for still we need his healing touch to perform these two ministries of love. It is no easy thing really to hear another person, really to attend his words and grasp their meaning, their power, their nuance, their pain. We say of the counselor, "All he did was listen!" But what an art, what a labor, what a skill that requires. To be understanding, open, and unthreatened as another reveals himself, to be secure and unafraid in the presence of emotional need—this is a ministry of grace and maturity that calls on all the personal powers we can muster. Afraid of our own inner selves and gripped by our own needs, we cannot admit the anguish of another, we cannot listen, we cannot hear.

Nor can we find the words of response, the words that communicate understanding, identification, liberation, and support. We are dumb before real needs, real openness, real honesty. Our need is as acute as this man's, our humanity is as impeded at his; we, too, cry to Jesus to open our ears and loose our tongues, to seize us —deaf and mute—and give us hearing and speech.

Open our ears and loose our tongues, O healing Christ, that we may hear the need of others and speak supportively in response.

WEDNESDAY MORNING
READING: MARK 8:11–13

"They asked him for a sign from heaven."

We ask for signs too; the whole risk of believing makes us very uncomfortable and we'd like it much better if we could get a clear, unambiguous sign from heaven. No way. A movie was produced some years back entitled *The Next Voice You Hear*. The idea was that suddenly an enormous voice would speak from the heavens all over the world in every language. It would say, "The next voice you hear will be the voice of God." Then God would speak and begin issuing commands and the like. It was not a box-office success, but I always liked the idea of the film because the voice of God device didn't work at all; people argued over whether it was really God or a hoax, and where they agreed that it was God they argued over what he had said; and where they agreed on what he had said, they argued over what it meant. And we were right back to square one.

There is no way God can give any more of a sign from heaven than he has given, no way he can reduce any further the risk of believing in him. We have to choose, and it's a chancy thing. This is one of the critical things human freedom does: it limits God's communication with us, it forces him to reach us in ambiguous ways, ways that admit of more than one interpretation. Otherwise he would be coercive, otherwise he would leave no room for faith.

Squirrels, cows, trees, and the like he communicates with clearly and cleanly, no ambiguity. Time to mate, they mate; time to leaf out, they leaf out; signs from heaven abound and there are no moral problems, no problems of choice. With us, it's different; we're on our own, we're free, and God always addresses us in a voice heard only by the ears of faith. Signs from heaven just aren't possible; signs cannot substitute for faith; that's part of being human, being moral, being free.

Help us to trust you, dear Lord, and to ask no more of you than you perceive us to need.

WEDNESDAY EVENING
READING: MARK 8:14–21

"You have eyes: can you not see?"

"Enable with perpetual light the dullness of our blinded sight."
These words open an ancient hymn frequently used in ordina-
tion services; I think of the Apostles each time I hear them. Oafs.
They all tumble into the boat to go somewhere and discover
they've forgotten the lunch. Jesus begins to speak of the subtle
ways temptations can overtake them, quietly and pervasively like
leaven, and they think he's scolding them because they left the
bread behind. I can see Jesus hang his head and shake it slowly
from side to side. "Good grief! Will they never catch on?"

He had called them, trained them, commissioned them; they
had gone out two by two on their first mission, they had returned
and reported to him all they had done and taught. These were not
novices; it wasn't as if they hadn't been schooled. Still this dense
and unthinking stupidity, this dullness of blinded sight.

We shouldn't be too hard on the Apostles for at least two reasons. One is that Jesus' explanation isn't all that helpful. Maybe
Mark has got two stories mixed here, but Jesus' questions leave me
as bewildered as the Apostles must have been. In the second place,
we twentieth-century apostles display the same slow comprehen-
sion, the same laboring imagination, the same dull wit. Thank
Heaven we are not saved by our own brilliance but by the Spirit's
enabling light; ordinations are a most appropriate occasion to be
reminded of this.

Enable with your Spirit's light the dullness of our blinded sight.

THURSDAY MORNING
READING: MARK 8:15

"Be on your guard against the leaven of the Pharisees and the leaven of Herod."

Jesus is looking far down the road as he issues this warning; little wonder his companions in the boat, worrying over the forgotten meal, miss his meaning. He sees a new community, a church, an institution taking shape around these men, and he perceives two dangers he must warn them of.

The leaven of the Pharisees is the danger of a new religious institution controlled by a new religious elite; the danger of the new community of God falling into the old hierarchical patterns. It's the most natural thing in the world, and history demonstrates it in every generation. We struggle with it still, this clericalization of leadership, this passing of control into the hands of the religious professionals. The leaven of the Pharisees infects the church today; energetic clergy and passive laity set the stage, both need the caution Jesus voices.

The leaven of Herod is the danger of a subverting alliance between church and state, church and culture, church and what contemporary American observers call "civil religion." The church is always tempted to capture the civil realm; almost always it turns out to be the captive. The advantages of establishment, even in America—tax-free status, prayer on civic occasion, God mottoes on currency and the like—rob us of our independence, domesticate us, tame us, make us the servants of the status quo and cheat us of our power to question and to protest.

Amazing that he could see these dangers from a rowboat on that ancient and tranquil lake; amazing that we hear him no better now than they did then.

Keep your church, Lord Jesus, on guard against every threat to our integrity and our independence; keep us loyal to you alone and to our calling in your kingdom.

THURSDAY EVENING
READING: MARK 8:27–33

"You are the Messiah."

An Italian film appeared a number of years ago, *The Gospel According to St. Matthew*. It was a literal and matter-of-fact rendition of that Gospel's narrative, acted largely by Italian peasants. For me it was a complete success. Peter's confession was depicted with particular realism and it captured, in a way I had never grasped, the preposterous character of this whole scene. Remember this is an itinerant teacher and healer, followed by a band of unprepossessing apprentices; the country folk receive him as a worthy rabbi, the establishment views him as a dangerous fool. To hear him called "the Messiah" would have alarmed both points of view, and to hear him respond as if this were an important secret would have confirmed his lunacy.

Centuries of piety have obscured this reality and made this episode seem reasonable and timely; the subsequent blindness of those closest to him betrays their failure to perceive what Peter confessed and how Jesus responded, or they might not have waited until the arrest to desert him. It is possible the entire exchange took place between Peter and Jesus alone, so little response do we get—here and subsequently—to this startling identification.

Puzzlement has greeted subsequent announcers of the messiahship of Jesus: Paul found it folly to the Greeks, a stumbling block to the Jews. Bewilderment still greets the proclamation that this distant healer is really present, that this gentle teacher is the Savior of the world, that this martyred idealist is the Son of the Most High God, that this carpenter's son is the Second Person of the Trinity. Like those who knew him first, the only answer for us to the unlikeliness of it all is to walk with him, to stay close, to listen, to watch, to persist. As surely as dawn follows darkness, clarity will come; as surely as sunshine warms the snow, our doubts will slowly melt away. Our experience will prove what our minds cannot encompass, and we will know, as they did, who he is.

Holy Jesus, we confess you as our Savior and our King; lead us to understand the meaning of our confession and to obey the demands of its truth.

FRIDAY MORNING
READING: MARK 8:34–38

"Anyone who wishes to be a follower of mine . . . must take up his cross, and come with me."

Jesus' definition of his own saviorhood is critical for us. Notice he sets out at once to persuade both his friends and "the people" that his manner of messiahship will be different. His talk takes them by surprise: In one sentence he is Messiah and in the next he is rejected, abused, and murdered. What kind of Messiah is that?

We are familiar with the politician who betrays a "messiah complex" and the conventional warning to hear him with caution. He is the office-seeker whose election will solve all problems and deliver us into a golden age of full employment, zero inflation, quality education, unspoiled environment, and no cavities. Our suspicion is well placed.

Jesus forswears this kind of extravagance; he is a Messiah without a messiah complex. He promises only what a latter-day realist promised: blood, sweat, and tears. No quick victory, no easy conquest, no instant paradise. Instead: Leave self behind . . . take up your cross . . . let yourself be lost for my sake. He will usher in a new era, oh yes, but not an era of easy irresponsibility, of careless, effortless nirvana; he promises no rose garden, at least none without the tilling, the planting, the feeding, the pruning.

Curious how we will force him into a role he so plainly renounces. We can take comfort that they did too: in their final earthly conversation with him, Luke records they asked with an edge of anxiety, "Is it now you're going to sweep it all aside and make things right?" The answer is no; not now, not ever. Grace, courage, support, forgiveness, love, endurance—all this he gives us. A world without problems, no.

We have taken up your Cross, Lord Jesus; suffer us not to let go, or to turn back.

FRIDAY EVENING
READING: MARK 8:34–35

"Whoever cares for his own safety is lost."

Jesus' ethical teaching has a remarkably pragmatic quality; we hear him saying, "Do such and such," not because it's nicer, or life will be better, but because the world is made that way and any other behavior is impossible. I see this about every biblical injunction, in fact, not just those of the Gospels.

It first came to me about cheating: the thing we need to be teaching our children is not that they shouldn't cheat but that they can't. There is no way to pull it off; you can't lie to life. You may deceive your teacher about what you know, but you can't deceive life; what you haven't learned leaves a hole that nothing but that learning can fill and no amount of covering over can disguise. Life won't be fooled. Life is created and sustained by Truth and it is the nature of Truth to forgive. It is not the nature of Truth to ignore, to hide, or to pretend.

He who saves his life will lose it; he who loses his life for my sake will find it. Jesus is simply stating fact. He's not saying, "Gee, life would certainly improve if more of us were more self-sacrificing," though that is demonstrably so. He's not saying, "It would be nicer if you'd think of others once in a while," though that is also accurate. He is saying, "When God made human life he made it in a particular way: made it so that a self-centered life produces misery, loneliness, and death, and so that a loving and generous life produces joy and fulfillment and peace. That's the way it is and there's no escaping that reality."

So often we think of religion as a body of assumptions abstracted from life, which will work for those who "believe." Not the religion of Jesus; his teaching is observation and description: Life is this way, God made it this way, it works this way. Get with it.

Turn us to you, Lord Christ, to see the world as you have made it, to hear the truth as you proclaim it, to order life as you direct it.

SATURDAY MORNING
READING: MARK 9:2–8

"In their presence he was transfigured."

Of course, there is relief from the harshness of life. Jesus doesn't promise us a rose garden, but he takes us into one once in a while. There is surcease, there is rest, refreshment, restoration. Within the week of his disclosing the grim and devastating fate that awaits him, he takes three of them to a hilltop, where they witness this extraordinary transformation. Jesus' figure becomes dazzling; there is light; voices are heard; other figures appear. The whole thing is staggering and moving; they are dumbfounded and fumble for an appropriate response.

Peter found his voice first, and with engaging and impulsive candor allowed as how this was a better place to be than that other and why couldn't they just stay? Why not build three tents for the actors in the drama and then just sit there and watch? We've been endlessly preached at about the temptations involved in mountaintop encounters with Jesus, when the work to be done lies below in the valleys, and I won't belabor that point. There is another temptation here and that is to put into concrete—tabernacles, booths, shelters, tents, however your version translates it—one experience of Jesus and then erect on that one experience an inflexible image of who he is, how he acts, and what he requires. We are tempted to arrest God's revelation at some level that holds particular meaning or satisfaction for us, and proceed with the rest of life as if God has nothing more to say to us, nothing more to disclose.

It helps me to think of doctrine as building a floor under our faith, to keep it from forgetting, from dropping back, from reverting down; rather than as a ceiling, which closes off more learning, fresh understanding, new realities, and new demands. "New occasions teach new duties," the hymnal sings: "Time makes ancient good uncouth; they must upward still and onward who would keep abreast of truth." God always has more to teach us, more of himself to show. The flash of revelation is never final, and we build tents on the mountaintops at the risk of being left behind by the surging current of God's self-disclosure.

Give us a vision of your beauty, O holy Jesus, and transform our hearts and our wills by its brightness.

SATURDAY EVENING
READING: MARK 9:14–29

"I have faith, help me where faith falls short."

This father is an authentic New Testament hero. Is there a Christian anywhere who can't identify with him? His declaration is unsurpassed for its unadorned honesty: I believe; help my unbelief. How tempted we are in the face of disaster to exaggerate our faith and our promises, to bargain loudly with the counterfeit of deathless gratitude and lifelong dedication. This father's desperation does not overcome his integrity: I believe and I don't believe, help me with that. That is some splendid kind of trust.

The absolution I grew up with addresses the confessed sinners in these words, "He pardoneth and absolveth all those who truly repent and unfeignedly believe . . ." "Truly repent" I could manage; "unfeignedly believe" used to bother me. I heard it saying, "who believe without blemish," "whose belief is untarnished with doubt," "who have no problems with faith," "whose trust is spontaneous and complete." The father in this story taught me that what God wants is faith without pretense, trust that is not fake, belief that does not feign perfection. God can accept that, he can use it, put it to work, make it heal. The phony protestations, born of crisis, simply get in his way, smoke up the atmosphere, cloud the issue, fog the lenses that would focus his power on human need.

God knows what's in us, we know he knows; to act out of any other reality is to make the ultimate denial, to display the ultimate distrust, to confess the ultimate unbelief. We cannot pretend with God; so often all he needs is our determination not to try.

Our faith is frail and in constant struggle, Lord; strengthen our belief and forgive our unbelief.

SUNDAY MORNING
READING: MARK 9:30–32

"The Son of Man is now to be given up into the power of men."

The shadow of the Cross has fallen visibly across Mark's narrative; we have Jesus making a secret journey, talking again of the fate that draws nearer, and the disciples now not only bewildered by his words but afraid to ask questions. It is a somber scene, quite unlike the enthusiastic crowds we're used to in Galilee.

I sense a couple of things about Jesus from this scant description—one is uncertainty. He reveals it in overtalking about his impending death, talk those around him don't understand and are frightened by. He is not moving them surely and supportively into an awareness of what is ahead, but rather indirectly, haltingly, obscurely. He is searching for a way to warn them and he doesn't find it, so his announcements are abrupt and unhelpful. This secret journey bothers me, too. Is he worried about timing? Is he trying to decide whether to wait it out? precipitate the confrontation? do it at Passover? some other time? Jesus is groping; the disciples sense this and are uneasy.

The other thing I sense is fear; fear not so much of death itself—that will surface later—but fear of failure. Fear that the denouement is coming too soon, that he is not ready, that the disciples are not ready, that poor timing could abort the whole thing; fear that there won't be time to finish, fear that the end will overtake him.

Well, I have been uncertain and, Lord knows, I've been afraid. Maybe if the Son of God has felt these gnawing, sleep-robbing, stomach-shrinking emotions, maybe he can save even me.

You have known fear and uncertainty, Lord Jesus; help us to bear ours as you bore yours.

SUNDAY EVENING
READING: MARK 9:33–37

"Whoever receives one of these children in my name receives me."

The ominous clouds of impending doom lift remarkably in this episode. Jesus, once again, is understanding, patient, cheerful, sure. He catches them in a foolish argument about their ranking within their own fellowship, but instead of accusing them of being childish, he uses a child to illustrate his teaching.

I can see them acting for all the world like children when he asks about their dispute; compounding the folly of it all as they glance in embarrassment from one to the other, waiting for someone to break the painful silence. But Jesus does not press; a word or two could demolish them in humiliation, but he refrains. There is weariness in the words "he sat down," but there is patience, too, and importance.

Instead of scolding them, he affirms them. He knew all along what the discussion was about, and he seizes that as an opportunity to teach them rather than to punish them. "If you want to be first," he says in effect, "there's something about that you need to know. You need to know that, the way God made the world, the servant of all is first." Once again, a reality observed rather than an injunction imposed; a statement of fact consistent with the other things he's said: The first shall be last and the last first; the meek shall inherit the earth; lose your life to save it.

Then he turns to the child and summons him into their midst. "If you want to be first," he goes on, "receive a child in my name. There is nothing a child can give you in return but gratitude, no way you can be repaid except in love. First place is reserved for that kind of uncalculating generosity, that kind of selfless service. See what I mean?"

You call us to serve without thought of reward, Master, and your own life is our best teacher.

Study Aids IV

A wider scene unfolds as Jesus' travels take him further from what has been his home base. Students of Mark have noticed striking similarities in the two accounts of journeys: 6:30–7:37, and 8:1–26. The parables are sufficient to suggest that Mark may have drawn on two sources, each of which contained a record of this trip, deciding to include both in order not to lose the details of either. There is wide agreement that he gives us duplicate accounts of a single feeding of a multitude.

The shadow of the Cross falls upon Mark's narrative in chapter 8, and the tone of the account is never the same. A thematic unity emerges after the drama of Peter's confession; his own death and the cost of discipleship dominate Jesus' words, and a certain severity can be felt in his mood. It's as if he has postponed revealing this darker side of his mission as long as he can; Peter's identification releases a torrent that has been held in check. The torrent begins with his announcement of the suffering, rejection, death, and resurrection that lie ahead. Jesus' dark mood comes to its first climax in the closing verses of chapter 9.

SUGGESTIONS FOR DISCUSSION AND REFLECTION:

Do our churches elevate human tradition over God's commandments? (7:8) Can you give examples? How can this be corrected?

What kind of signs do we ask Jesus for? (8:11–12)

Why do you suppose Jesus led this blind man "out of the village" to heal him? (8:23) Why did Mark record this detail?

Do you sometimes feel like the twelve, not understanding what Jesus says? (8:21, 33; 9:10) Is there some particularly puzzling statement of Jesus' in this section?

What externals get in our way as Christians and church members today? (7:14–23)

What kinds of crosses does Jesus lay on our shoulders?(8:34)

Why did Jesus select these three to witness his transfiguration? (9:2; see also 5:37)

What purpose was served by the Transfiguration? (9:2–13)

FIFTH WEEK

MONDAY MORNING
READING: MARK 9:38–50

"He who is not against us is on our side."

The generosity of Jesus' mood carries into his next response. Asked about outsiders who use his name, he makes a really quite sweeping statement: he who is not against us is on our side. Can he really mean that? It's a quite different thing from saying it the other way: he who is not with me is against me. It would seem in the former that all the apathetic are counted with him; in the latter they're all against him. In any case, Jesus' mood is generous and expansive and he reaches out a wide embrace: "If you're not my enemy you're my friend." I like it that way; so much of the time not being his enemy is the best I can do.

But that kindly spirit dissipates suddenly, and we're not quite prepared for the severity of the denunciations that close this discourse. Imagine! Speaking tenderly of childhood in one breath and advising self-mutilation in the next. A sudden urgency and anger well up from somewhere and explode across this monologue. But this is the Jesus of the closing chapters—harbingers that appeared first in his words have now spread to his mood and demeanor.

The knot of tension is tightening in this tale, and we see over Jesus' shoulder a gathering storm.

Keep us close to you, dear Lord; do not abandon us to our wandering attention, our thin commitment, our fragile enthusiasm.

MONDAY EVENING
READING: MARK 10:1–12

"What God has joined together, man must not separate."

Again, an adamant Jesus. At the first question, he closes the gap Moses left; indoors, to his disciples, he dispels any lingering doubt about leniency. We have come to an age in which no Christian body I know of puts this rigid requirement into pastoral practice; what authority, then, is left to Jesus in the matter of marriage?

Two observations: He's speaking harshly about everything at this point, and we must be cautious about erecting these responses into law. I've never heard anyone propose legislating his advice about cutting off your hand if it offends you; in fact, we recoil in horror from reports of such punishment for thievery. Jesus is not enacting a code of law; in fact, he's replacing a code of law with the Gospel of forgiveness and redemption. We dare not isolate these exacting standards from that reality. The early Church soon learned that exclusion from fellowship of those who caved in under persecution was a thoroughly inappropriate and sub-Christian response, despite words of Jesus' that could be used in support of such severity.

In the second place, Jesus is speaking of a situation in which divorce was easy and totally demeaning to women. The question reflects the realities: Men divorced women, not the other way around, and did it by handing them a piece of paper. There was no place in that culture for an unmarried woman; divorce put a woman into the street. In his answer he elevates marriage as lifelong and binding, and defines divorce in the strongest word he can use: adultery. And in a further and most subtle way, he elevates the role of women by giving them equal status in the marriage contract: the right of each party to a faithful spouse is affirmed in his response to the questions of his disciples.

No one gets married to get divorced; I've never known a marriage that didn't at least begin with Jesus' ideal and with his expectation of permanence.

Infuse our marriages, O God, with loyalty and caring, and make our homes places of gentleness and mutual respect.

TUESDAY MORNING
READING: MARK 10:13–27

"The Kingdom of God belongs to such as these."

What is it about children we find so disarming? Their ready delight? Their bottomless energy? Their simplicity? Their complexity? Their toughness? Their vulnerability? It's tempting to romanticize, I know; men eager to be grandfathers are an easy mark. But let's take Jesus at his word and discover what it is about the Kingdom of God that belongs to childhood.

Children take life as it comes. An author spent fifteen months in a polio ward, the only adult among those stricken cripplingly by a disease we have now conquered. He focused his observations on the parents who came visiting, and he discovered them more disturbed, more depressed, more shattered by their children's affliction than were the children themselves. He decided the parents' dreams of the future had been destroyed and that the children had no such vulnerability because their future was unplanned, unimagined, left to itself. The outlines of a child's future are blurred, but its color is trust. That means the openness of the future is indefinite rather than uncertain, an immense difference.

Jesus points up that difference in his next encounter. A stranger asks for the key to eternal life and Jesus, warmed by the sincerity of his inquiry, counsels renunciation and offers a place in his band. The stranger's face fell; his future was mapped out and it included no such revolution. The outlines of his future were specific and its color was caution; the adventure of the kingdom of God is forfeit to the promise of an earthly security.

Thus does the openness of the child make folly of the prudence of the adult.

Help us to place our future in your hands, good Lord, and to live each day with childhood's trust and delight.

TUESDAY EVENING
READING: MARK 10:28–31

"Many who are first will be last and the last first."

There is a story told about a Benedictine monk, musing on the virtues of the various orders of the Roman Church. "Well," he allowed, "the Franciscans beat us in good works, and the Dominicans beat us in scholarship, but nobody can beat us in humility!" I am reminded of that boast when I read Peter's words, pointing out the perfection of the disciples' renunciation.

Jesus was magnanimous in his response, reassuring beyond my understanding. Perhaps Peter was really down and needed stroking; maybe Jesus sensed a real depression in his otherwise ebullient disciple and administered the tonic of a glowing reward: in this age a hundredfold return of houses, families, land. But right in the middle he makes a curious reversal; without breaking stride he adds "and persecutions besides . . . many who are first will be last . . ."

For the Benedictine, the warning that boasted humility becomes pride; for Peter, that boasted renunciation becomes prudent investment. It won't wash; motives emerge, the truth comes out, God is not mocked. Put yourself last in order to be first, and you will find yourself among the first who will be last.

Keep us straight in our motives for serving you, Lord Christ, and where we cannot be selfless in our motivation, keep us honest about our sin.

WEDNESDAY MORNING
READING: MARK 10:32–45

"Can you drink the cup that I drink?"

Again, the disciples awed and fearful; again, Jesus pointing to the darkening horizon. Mark draws tighter the threads of his narrative, lifting our eyes and our attention to what we know lies ahead.

Somehow, James and John have missed it, missed the word to Peter, missed an awful lot of what's been going on and what's been said. They want to be senior vice-presidents. Yes, thank you very much, they're quite ready, quite able, quite willing to accept Jesus' fate and share his lot, to suffer his baptism and drink his cup. Jesus must have smiled at their innocence. "Well, ready you may be," he answers, "but what you ask is not mine to give."

The others get wind of it and Jesus rephrases the teaching he has given them earlier. This time he caps it with the irrefutable illustration: Look at me. If you want to see what it means to be the absolute top of the heap, look at the Son of Man, a servant, a ransom for every wasted, wretched human life.

Every Christian witness has to have this element, has to share to some visible degree this testimony: Look at me, my life displays what my words argue. That's the litmus of our authenticity, that's the baptism we share, that's the cup he summons us to drink.

Make us your faithful witnesses, O Lord, by giving us the grace to live faithful lives.

WEDNESDAY EVENING
READING: MARK 10:46–52

"I want my sight."

Bartimaeus, one of my favorites. He reminds me how important names are, individuality, people. For all his brevity, Mark alone among the Gospel writers records this blind beggar's name. We don't know why, and it doesn't really matter to me. What does matter to me is that Mark does name him and I take that as a small testimony to a very large truth: each of us, one at a time, is important to Jesus.

Bartimaeus asks for his sight and at Jesus' word it is restored. The difference between us and this blind beggar is striking: it is the contrast between vision and sight. Recognition has to do with vision; seeing has to do with sight. Bartimaeus had the vision to recognize Jesus; he asked for his sight to see. We have the sight to see and ask for the vision to recognize.

So often sight gets in the way of vision. Wasn't it Milton who said, "I thank God who took away my sight, that my soul might see"? Speaking of the workings of his own mind, Albert Schweitzer said of himself, "I thank God that he did not make me brilliant; it has forced me to be profound." Eyesight so filled with the details of the foreground can miss the reality that lies behind it; failing to see the forest for the trees, that kind of thing.

So we sighted come, like Bartimaeus, begging what we need: vision, awareness, sensitivity, recognition. Asking that, beyond the shape and surface of things, our hearts be opened to the truth, the reality, the presence.

Open the eyes of our souls, O God, to see your gracious hand in all your works to delight in your presence in every moment, to lift our hearts and wills in glad obedience.

THURSDAY MORNING
READING: MARK 11:1–11

"Hosanna! Blessings! Hosanna in the heavens!"

Palm Sunday. My first course in New Testament punctured two illusions: Palms don't grow in Jerusalem (too high), and the size of this parade has been exaggerated. The average church probably fields a Palm Sunday congregation that would double this procession. Mark isn't responsible; he mentions neither palms nor crowds. Nothing distorts like nostalgia, and centuries of piety have been fond of this day.

It was big enough, to be sure; big enough to be noticed. The New English Bible heads these pages "Challenge to Jerusalem," and that's what Jesus is doing: throwing down the gauntlet, calling attention to his presence, claiming the royalty of the prophesied king who comes meek, riding on a donkey. It was a bold stroke, not overlooked by those who believed in him, those who feared him, or those who plotted against him.

"Our Master needs it"—claim or code? We can make of this a moving lesson in stewardship, the surrender of something of value to the simple claim of Jesus' need. That it might have been a code is possible, too. John's Gospel is full of a Jerusalem ministry; it never appears in the others. We have in Mark only hints that Jesus had disciples in the Holy City unknown to the Galilean followers; this is one. A colt tied by prearrangement, a password prearranged? "Give the colt to the man who says, 'Our Master needs it.'" Remember, he said to be wise as serpents and harmless as doves.

There is so much about these years we don't know; all Mark relates could transpire in about six weeks. We close the door firmly on any but the most modest speculation. We know enough to crown him King; anything more we really need, he can tell us himself.

O Jesus, this day we hail you King; help us make you King in our attitudes and our decisions.

THURSDAY EVENING
READING: MARK 11:12–14, 20–24

"May no one ever again eat fruit from you!"

Another puzzler. Jesus cursed the tree and doubtless no one ever ate its fruit again. But it didn't die; we've wrestled with it ever since, wondering why he did it, hoping it wasn't just a cranky mood or a fit of pique. Mark can make nothing of it himself, and compounds the mystery by explaining Jesus found no figs because it wasn't fig season.

Why he did it baffles me still; that he did it no longer strikes me as incredible. The mystery of the physical world, once banished by a prematurely optimistic (and unscientific) scientism, is creeping back, perhaps I should say flooding back. We recognize that those descriptions we call natural laws are operational in only very limited arenas and that the further we look into the heavens beyond and the atom within, the more we are driven to poetry, metaphor, allusion. And the more room there is for strange connections between living things, the more legitimacy there is for mystery in healing and disease and recovery.

People talk to plants, you know, even these days. People who are otherwise unrecognizable and do quite normal things. Yes, even sing to them. Kooky? Once I might have said so, but no more. There seem to be some little-understood, poorly conceptualized links between living things, even across that old animal-vegetable barrier.

If your stockbroker or your son's math teacher talk to their plants, why not Jesus?

———————————

Open our minds, O Lord, to the mystery of all of life, to the wonder and the majesty of all that you have made.

FRIDAY MORNING
READING: 11:15–19

"He began driving out those who bought and sold in the temple."

Commerce in the holy place; how cautious we must be. The jokes about bazaars and bingo, rummage sales and car washes all betray a real uneasiness about religion and money. For all that, money is essential to the existence of the Church; and for all that, the giving of it is essential to our souls' health. Because the holiest realities are involved, opportunities for abuse and exploitation abound.

Jesus left a dramatic lesson, a violently acted parable. Money changers there had to be, since the coin of the Roman realm was not acceptable in the alms basins of the Jewish Temple. But apparently some took advantage; maybe the whole scheme was at base a rip-off. Pigeons had to be sold somewhere; they were required for sacrifice and some source had to be arranged. Again, there may have been overpricing or gouging or kickbacks to the priests. Jesus was outraged by it all and, in his only display of physical anger, simply cleaned out the whole forecourt of the temple. The crowd was spellbound by this display and the priests and their cohorts scared to death.

The burst of temper completed what Sunday's parade had begun. The die is cast, the whole thing is getting out of hand, something has to be done. The antagonists are on a collision course and there is no turning back; each evening sees the climax one day nearer. Momentum gathers, inexorable as the tide swelling in flood; we are borne along on the crest of this current as it races toward Calvary and the fulcrum of history. This is that heavy week we have ever since called Holy.

We watch with foreboding the storm clouds that gather over the Holy City; keep us faithful, Lord Jesus, as we walk with you these final days.

FRIDAY EVENING
READING: MARK 11:27–33

"The baptism of John: was it from God, or from men?"

An edge of antagonism creeps into Jesus' voice in this exchange; little wonder, given the events of the day before. The question of his adversaries is surely what one would expect, and I imagine Jesus had prepared this trap of his own.

The crowd apparently is still with Jesus; at least the temple authorities fear to antagonize them. Passover passions are beginning to build and the temple partisans must sense that, aroused now, those passions would attach to Jesus against them. This whole chafing patriotism that surfaced every spring against the hated Romans had to be carefully manipulated away from Jesus and into the service of the ecclesiastical establishment. They had their time-table, too, and this encounter could not be allowed to escalate into premature confrontation.

Jesus' question is so clever we overlook its profounder dimensions; the question of God's authority versus man's runs through more of our choices than we might like to admit. It isn't always an ultimate thing, like Bonhoeffer's choice to defy Hitler's government; it can be little things like popularity, social acceptability, the pressure to conform. And yet, little things lead to big things; small choices pave the way, set the direction, establish the pattern.

Can we answer his question about John any better than they?

Teach us to be faithful in small things, O Lord, that the larger decisions of life may find us obedient and trustworthy.

SATURDAY MORNING
READING: MARK 12:1–12

"He will give his vineyard to others."

The strategy of Holy Week seems to involve taking the initiative. In the Palm Sunday march, the angry scene at the temple (a friend of mine calls it his "temple tantrum"), the turning around of the question about authority—in each instance Jesus has taken the initiative in his own hands and chosen his own ground. He does it here, with this thinly disguised recapitulation of Jewish history.

Two things strike me: God always finds someone to send, some fool willing to speak for him, to represent him, to stake his claim. Do you remember that poignant song by the Beatles, "The Fool on the Hill"? "The fool on the hill sees the sun going down and the eyes in his head see the world spinning round . . . nobody seems to notice and nobody seems to care . . ." It seems there's always someone ready to face abuse, rejection, stoning, death. When God cries out, "Whom shall I send and who will go for us?" someone always answers, "Send me."

The second is about Jesus' audience: their own guilt condemns them. So easy for them to claim, "Yes, there are even more false prophets than true, and we are protecting God's vineyard from fraudulant claimants." Their own guilt silences them. They could have responded, "No good thing can come from Nazareth, and you are just the latest in a long line of rabble-rousing, wonder-working malcontents." No, their protests are cut off by the constrictions of guilt in their own throats. So painfully do they see the finger of history pointed at them, their hearts freeze and their voices dry up.

I think Judgment Day will be like this for all of us; a recitation of the wretched history of the response of God's people to God's prophets is all that will be needed. Like theirs, our silence will enter our plea of guilty.

We stand mute before your judgment seat, O God; our only claim is your mercy.

SATURDAY EVENING
READING: MARK 12:13–17

"Master, you are an honest man."

I am impressed with the obsequious address of his tormentor; it has the ring of truth in it and a kind of grudging respect. I wonder. I wonder if deep down in the heart of the chosen spokesman for this attempt to impugn him there wasn't a responsive chord Jesus had struck, a tiny, subversive spark of admiration, a buried yearning to hear more of what he said, to linger on the fringes of his discourse, to learn a little more of what he's like. Could be. He didn't press Jesus very hard; one question is all he asked. And, actually, he let Jesus off rather easily.

Jesus' response is designed to silence the questioner rather than to answer the question; it leaves enormous gaps in the issue of what belongs to whom. Caesar's "possession" of anything is precisely like ours: derivative, transient, reversionary. All is God's; what seems to be ours is lent only for a season and must be returned with an accounting. All the ultimates belong to God; anything else in the way of government or commerce is a temporary arrangement for convenience and must stand aside when it ceases to serve the Creator or begins to violate the Creation.

We have here only a half-hearted thrust, and Jesus turns it aside with half a parry. He may even have smiled at his antagonist, recognizing a miscast enemy. I have a notion the "enemy" smiled back, recognizing a misrepresented friend.

All things are yours, Heavenly Father; make us wise and generous stewards over all you lend us, and keep our "possessions" from possessing us.

SUNDAY MORNING
READING: MARK 12:18–27

"God is not God of the dead but of the living."

The next question—it's the Sadducees' turn this time—is better constructed; they've done their homework and they're trying to stick to something they have convictions about. They have confected a situation that strains credulity and would break the back of the most inclusive and detailed construction of the hereafter. But that sort of thing delights the aggressive theologian: he loves to defend his conclusions in the most outrageous circumstances and to press his opponents' assumptions against the wall of his own brilliantly inventive argument. It's all a game and harmless enough most of the time. Like ice hockey, it's played on a very fast and a very thin surface and is without redeeming social value outside the rink. The game of theological debate suffers the same inflation of significance as other spectator sports; life goes on outside the stadium largely unaffected by the passionate shouting within. Fun for the theologians, if they manage to take their theology seriously without taking themselves seriously.

Jesus doesn't give it the time of day. The whole preposterous question is beside the point, since marriage is a sacramental relationship here that has never been responsibly thought to survive death. The personal intertwining of lives, yes; the particular arrangements of marriage, no.

Jesus does pick up on their unspoken disbelief in the Resurrection, and silences them with a neat piece of rabbinical legerdemain. More important issues preoccupy him; one is the bait offered by the next fisherman to venture into these risky waters.

Keep us, O God of truth, from dissipating our energies in conjecture; help us to focus them in obedience.

SUNDAY EVENING
READING: MARK 12:28–34

"Which commandment is first of all?"

Next the lawyers, and we can be encouraged that one finds himself moving toward the kingdom at the end of the conversation. Aggressive as Jesus is in this mounting tension, he is still open to finding a responsive ear, a receptive heart.

"Which commandment is first of all?" Well, it's human nature to boil things like commandments down to their essence, to condense life's requirements into brief, memorizable summaries. At the end of Paul's hymn to love, he selects three human activities to "abide," and chooses one to label "greatest." We're always trying to do that. The problem is that as the statements get shorter the words get larger; the only way life's realities can be expressed in short sentences is by large words, words like faith and hope and love.

So here Jesus uses four words to answer the request for the most important command: love, God, neighbor, and self. Each one a word of enormous scale, shadowy borders, and mysterious depths. The realities of life the way God created it require such words; words that raise more questions than they answer, words that open out, words that indicate rather than define, words that point rather than enclose.

So we wrestle still in word and deed with what he requires of us and how he means to work in our lives and what our obedience involves. But talking and doing are two different things, and each has its own requirement. The definition of God's command requires immense generalities; the doing of his command requires small specifics.

Seize us in your measureless love, O God, and set us to your smallish tasks of neighborhood and self.

Study Aids V

The story is approaching its climax and the pace of the narrative quickens. Jesus is on his final journey and he enters Jerusalem for the last time. In Mark's account, this is Jesus' only visit to the Holy City. Passover fever runs high; Jerusalem is jammed with pilgrims and tense with excitement.

Chapter 10 embraces the last of Jesus' general teaching; he speaks of marriage and children, the obstacles and rewards of discipleship, the call to service. Aside from his response to James and John, the shadow of the cross seems to lift for a moment.

The triumphal entry—an event of increasing liturgical popularity—marks another turning point; events and discourse reveal again the ominous clouds that gather over Jerusalem. Jesus storms the Temple commerce, curses the fig tree and sidesteps the question of authority. He relates the long accusatory parable of the wicked tenants and finds himself baited by spokesmen from each party that opposes him.

SUGGESTIONS FOR DISCUSSION AND REFLECTION:

What relevance does Jesus' response to the "outsider" have for the ecumenical movement? (9:38–41) What practical obstacles existed then? now?

Most of us do not have "great wealth"; what kinds of things do we cling to? (10:22)

Is all divorce wrong? Who can decide? (10:1–12)

Can the church sanction marriages that are in intention less than lifelong? (10:1–12)

Have you sacrificed something really important for your discipleship? (10:28)

Do we spoil God's house of prayer today? In what ways? (11:17)

How does faith affect sickness? (10:52) Other aspects of life? (11:22–24)

How much of faith is personal and how much intellectual?

What does Jesus mean by the kingdom of God? (12:34, 10:24)

Did you overlook Mark's echo of the Lord's Prayer in 11:25–26?

SIXTH WEEK

MONDAY MORNING
READING: MARK 12:38–40

"Beware of the doctors of the law."

The sins of the Church; they are really not so different today from what they were then. Erecting buildings in the name of Jesus and conducting business on behalf of his kingdom doesn't change human nature that much. It is part of the relevance of the Bible that we are still largely the same and create for ourselves the same kinds of problems. *Plus ça change, plus c'est la même chose,* the French say; the more things change, the more they stay the same. Those who won't learn from history are condemned to repeat it, Santayana adds.

Institutions remain cumbersome and inert, easily seduced by their own self-interest, preoccupied with their own survival. It's a melancholy and ubiquitous fact of life that once an ideal, any ideal, becomes institutionalized, confusion sets in between the accomplishment of the ideal and the aggrandizement of the institution. These men Jesus points to are not rapacious and vile; they are simply trapped in this demonic confusion. We have to face it: larger church budgets do not necessarily mean more Christianity, any more than larger hospital bills necessarily mean better health care.

Jesus' warning is stern: the power of established religion to undermine human values is immense. The distinctive garb of religious prestige and the respectful salutations it attracts—these have really very little to do with God's priorities of humility and love and justice. Beware the power of successful religion to distort the real values; every such institution needs its revolutionaries like Jesus, and they make the powerful of their generations just as uncomfortable as he made the powerful of his.

Keep before your Church, O Lord, the single calling that gives it life, and protect us from the seduction of secondary preoccupation.

MONDAY EVENING
READING: MARK 12:41–44

"A poor widow dropped in two tiny coins."

More about Church and money, and again little has changed. Givers are ostentatious and anonymous, sacrificial and superficial, cheerful and churlish, in any of the multiple combinations those descriptions provide. We know this widow combines the good in two. She is anonymous and sacrificial, and we trust that without a cheerful demeanor she wouldn't have attracted Jesus' notice.

The realities of Church giving Jesus perceived in the widow's offering are the realities that obtain today; for all the improvements that have been made in the area of stewardship, the truths inherent in this episode are still critical. (It ought to be said that every policy or device that increases dollar results is not necessarily an improvement.) First, only God and you know what your giving means to you. No one else can understand the dynamics behind the individual decision we make on that pledge card or in that envelope; that is so because that act involves so many of our values and our attitudes, so much of our history and our hope. Only you and God can know the mood and the motivation that produces that choice.

The second truth Jesus preserves for us here is that the significance of your gift lies right there in that decision; it's what it means to you. Significance is not measured by purchasing power or size in relation to need; the meaning of gifts of money lies between the money and the giver and nowhere else. Size makes a difference, one gift builds a library and another buys a book; there's a difference and an important difference. But the meaning of the gift, that lies not in what it buys but in where it originated, how it relates to the heart and life and spirit of the giver.

Jesus makes it plain: to understand the meaning of the offering, look not at the gift but at the giver. Even then, unless you are God, that meaning remains the giver's secret.

Transform our greed to gratitude, Lord Jesus; replace our caution with generosity.

TUESDAY MORNING
READING: MARK 13:1–2

"Not one stone will be left upon another."

I have a friend who loudly inquires, when the conversation gets a little sticky, "Seen any red-winged blackbirds lately?" Another friend confesses his family has a code that means "Change the subject!" It's a kind of versicle and response that goes like this: "I think we'll get some rain this week." "Hope it doesn't wipe out the rhubarb crop!"

I think of these deliberate diversions when I read this pointless remark to Jesus: "What huge stones! What huge buildings!" I wonder how these words got remembered across all the years they waited to be written down. There must have been a heavy silence that cried out to be filled, or maybe Mark invented them to introduce Jesus' observation about time and temples. Robert Frost wrote a poem that begins "Something there is that doesn't love a wall," and other sages before and after Jesus have prophesied, "This too will pass—these monuments, so grand to us, will one day feed the fascination of the archeologist."

Sic transit gloria mundi; how fleeting the world's glory! How fleeting all time, how quickly it passes, like sand between our fingers, and is forever gone. Permanence we must find elsewhere, in truth, for instance; in beauty; in goodness; in achievement; in love and spirit—values beyond the ravages of time, fashioned of the material of eternity, written and sealed in the heart of God. Those stately mansions of the soul will last; not stones and buildings.

Lift our eyes, O God, to the works of eternity, knowing the frailty of the monuments of time.

TUESDAY EVENING
READING: MARK 13:3–22

"When will this happen? What will be the sign?"

The little apocalypse, Biblical scholars call this chapter, or some specific parts of it. It is an amalgam of authentic words of Jesus and material drawn from the tradition that produced the Book of Revelation. That tradition is a literary form unfamiliar and opaque to us; this chapter in Mark represents a mild example of the style. The Book of Revelation contains apocalyptic at its most extravagant and arcane. Esoteric though this may be, it is not useless to us; its appearance in Mark betrays how early the church either underwent or feared persecution and what kinds of assurances Christians found supportive.

Notice that the apocalyptic section begins with typical human curiosity about God's timetable and that Jesus' first response is "Do not be misled!" Jesus is typically cautious about conjecture and while he seems willing to talk about what lies ahead his emphasis is caution and readiness, the disposition of the person within rather than the sequence of events without. He puts the whole picture on a long scale and sees much history unfolding before any drastic changes come. "Don't be alarmed . . . be on your guard" are watchwords for the long pull. We don't hear him say, "Synchronize your watches."

He foresees persecution and betrayal; he's experienced that already and knows more lies immediately ahead. There's a human touch in his hoping it won't come in winter. He warns about false messiahs in the same breath he speaks of a sudden end and concludes it all by confessing he doesn't really know, only the Father.

He remains true to his reluctance to lift the veil of the future. As when he admitted children to his presence and embraced them in a happier time, he turns us back to our only weapon against the future: trust. "My words will never pass away."

Keep our faith rooted in you, Lord Jesus, and independent of the vagaries of human speculation.

WEDNESDAY MORNING
READING: MARK 13:32–37

"I say to everyone: Keep awake."

A word about readiness: You do not know when the master of the house is coming. Much of my inner reflection centers around my freedom, and about the disparity between my conviction that we can always choose for Christ if we want to and my experience that it is possible to lose that desire. At the point when we lose that desire to respond to Christ we lose our freedom and enter bondage to whatever it is we put ahead of God.

The most poignant illustration I know of this is alcoholism. It seems to me that, in the progress of that addiction, the alcoholic passes on some day, with some drink, a point of no return, a point beyond which he can never manage alcohol again. Probably that point is never subsequently identifiable, even though that person later achieves sobriety; but it was there that the master of the house came and found him careless, inattentive, unready.

These pleasures and pursuits of ours that take control of us— alcohol, money, sex, success, possessions—give us no warning when they are about to conquer us. It's always by hindsight that we discover that somewhere along the line we surrendered and the battle was lost; we traded places, and what was my servant became my master, what was my possession became my possessor.

Keep awake, Jesus warns; it is a subtle and pernicious process by which we forfeit our freedom. Watch. Evening or midnight, cockcrow or early dawn, you'll learn of his visit only after he's come and gone.

O master of our house, keep us watchful and alert for your coming; guard us from carelessness and inattention.

WEDNESDAY EVENING
READING: MARK 14:1–2

"The chief priests and the doctors of the law were trying to devise some cunning plan."

Wednesday. Passover two days off, tensions high and climbing, prudence counsels we wait until the festival is over to avoid rioting. What happened to this scheme? Why didn't they wait? Did these officials change their mind? Did Jesus force their hand? Was there a sudden change of heart in the populace? Did Barabbas suddenly appear as a decoy for the people's patriotism?

We know very little and much conjecture, pious and otherwise, has focused on the sequence of these events, the mechanisms that brought trial and execution to pass, the machinations of the chief protagonists, the balance of innocence and guilt among Judas, Jews, and Romans. It may be that Mark reports only a single proposal from a long discussion or the conclusion of only one of a number of such consultations. A couple of things we do know: there was specific and murderous plotting against him, and Jesus knew it.

He may have provoked it, he may have ignored it; he did nothing to protect himself from it. He sensed early on that it would end this way, and he must have set himself some tasks that needed to be done first. I believe he's satisfied that he has done what he can, that he's brought the soon-to-be Apostles about as far as he can. In John's Gospel, he tells them "It is expedient for you that I go away."

The tale tightens to its climax and he is ready.

We watch with apprehension as the enemy conspires; we draw strength, Lord Jesus, from your quiet and your calm.

THURSDAY MORNING
READING: MARK 14:3–9

"She broke it open and poured the oil over his head."

The first thing that strikes me about this event is the overreaction of the disciples; I wonder what lay behind it. It seems there must have been episodes of abuse or rejection or apathy, which might have stirred some hostility in them, but Mark uses this extreme language nowhere else to describe the disciples: "Some . . . said to one another angrily . . . they turned upon her with fury . . ." Were they imagining his death was not imminent? Were they still unused to the impious and the outcast? Were they jealous of this gesture of love and the pleasure it gave Jesus? Surely Jesus, by now, had no reputation left to protect.

I'm grateful he let her do this; I delight in the easy way he accepted her extravagance. I've learned, from my own experience with the gratitude of people, that our response to it is a clue to our self-esteem. I've had to learn how to welcome sincerely offered praise, and I know it relates to my learning to accept myself as a worthy person. Strange what low self-esteem does to us; it makes us both seek praise and then turn it aside, reach for it and reject it. Among the things guilt destroys is our ability to appreciate authentic admiration, our capacity to let ourselves be loved; feelings of unworthiness are somehow not soothed by gestures of affection, they are uncovered, stirred, awakened.

Such self-disesteem did not plague Jesus; his easy appreciation of this anointing confirms that humility is not self-abasement, that the opposite of egotism is not self-hatred. Jesus had what we would call today a strong ego structure; I'm glad, because it's one of the things he can give me that I need most of all.

I believe, Lord Jesus, that no person you hold dear deserves contempt; teach me that I myself am numbered among them.

THURSDAY EVENING
READING: MARK 14:10-11

"Then Judas Iscariot . . . went to the chief priests to betray him."

The first and only Passion play I've ever seen came to the town I was serving in the early 1950s; it was an elaborate and energetically promoted event and I came away with very mixed feelings. The part of Jesus was grossly overacted and the other characters were all cardboard. All except one, Judas; the one believable human being on that stage that night was Judas. That performance began my long conjecture about this character and about his role in the whole drama of Jesus' public ministry and its climax on Good Friday. Conjecture about Judas has a history that reaches into the Gospel records themselves; attempts to account for him and for Jesus' selection of him adorn other accounts of this narrative, which Mark is content to leave barren of explanation. None of the conventional answers to the questions Judas raises commends itself to me and I'm unable to invent anything more plausible. I do claim one conviction: he is human, no more venal or vicious than the others, motivated by the same kind of mixture that drives us all, cursed with a weakness of some sort that has got him singled out to be the universal symbol of betrayal and deception. Peter's denial has been forgiven; the desertion of the others finds pardon; why not Judas?

Maybe we can say he quit too soon: the patron saint of all of us who can't face the consequences of our bad decisions, who give in to despair, who feel no one has ever sinned as we have, no one's ruination has ever been so contemptible and unspeakable as ours. I hope Judas has found forgiveness; I hope he has faced Jesus and discovered it is not the end. If he has, I hope word gets around; there are so many of us like him.

Your love is large, O Lord, and your embrace is wide; there is no sin that can exceed or escape them.

FRIDAY MORNING
READING: MARK 14:12–16

"So they prepared the Passover."

Here is another hint of a Jerusalem ministry and a band of disciples unknown to the Galileans. This just had to be an arrangement: "Go into the city and a man will meet you." Mark's record of even these intensive days leaves many hours unaccounted for. Still it is curious that Jesus would keep two groups of intimates separated, and even more curious that there was any need to. It does seem an elaborate scenario to accomplish so simple a thing; recognition devices and passwords seem foreign to Jesus' way of doing.

The guide's recognition device of a water pot on the shoulder was an embarrassing badge of male domestication, and hence reliably conspicuous. I think about those unique souls who willingly suffer embarrassment in order to make their witness. Salvation Army bands playing to audiences they outnumber, Watchtower vendors vainly peddling their doom, Hari-Krishnas in cadence and costume. There must be a special place for them in heaven. My seminary class decided to do some street preaching in Berkeley and I found it the toughest thing I ever tried; an inhibited and halting performance forever disqualifies this witness from that happy corner of paradise.

But the unidentified Passover courier is there; he shouldered his burden of humiliation and made his way faithfully past the snickers and snorts that must have greeted him in the crowded streets, accepting his assignment and its strange requirement. Little did he know, I suppose, how long and profoundly remembered, how frequently and fervently reenacted that fateful supper would be.

Help us lift high our witness, Lord Christ; if not always with joy, then, like this courier, with fidelity and determination.

FRIDAY EVENING
READING: MARK 14:22–25

"During supper he took bread."

Food and love—inseparable. Three strangers appear at the door of Abraham's tent and he sends Sarah to knead some dough and make cakes; Jesus is heading for Bethany and Martha busies herself at the cooking fire; I once ate chicken Kiev at four in the afternoon because my parishioner's appreciation of my pastoral call took that unrefusable form. Food and love go together. Do you remember the awkwardness of a silent meal opposite a stranger in the dining car? Do you avoid the fast-food arrangements that seat people at a shelf facing a wall? Ulcers have been described to me as a stomach persuaded it is starving because the heart feels no love. Nearly every church I know has two places to gather and eat: church for food from the Lord's Table, parish hall for food from the kitchen. Maybe they should never have been separated.

I believe all these connections between food and love trace back to our first gratification of need in the close warmth and flowing food of our mother's breast. We encounter our first satisfaction of those most fundamental needs—food and love—in the same experience; we are fondled and we are fed. The quality and texture of these needs change as we mature; we move from milk to other foods, from receiving love as infants to loving and being loved as adults. But life requires food and life requires love—our need of them is both our first and our final experience.

So natural then, that the King of Love would take bread and wine from the table of their friendship, and, gathering up every act of hospitality, every experience of love and food, would command us to eat and remember him.

At every table, in every meal, help us to see the generosity of your hand, most giving God, and to feel the warmth of your love.

SATURDAY MORNING
READING: MARK 14:26–31

"After singing the Passover hymn, they went out to the Mount of Olives."

Remember the singing of "Nearer My God to Thee" as the *Titanic* went down? Watching the lifeboats pull away, those left behind linked arms on that steeply tilting deck and sustained their courage in song. That tragedy and this are not dissimilar. A menacing cloud hangs over this supper; Jesus has spoken of shedding his own blood, the betrayer has stolen away, the mood is ominous. Like those *Titanic* victims, they sing a hymn to confess their common fear and to claim their common support.

Jesus knows how fragile their bravery is and how quickly the hesitation of one will become the panic of all. Peter's pitiful protest sets the tone for the whole; they are filled with the sense of brotherhood and the strength of shared determination. All the more startling the sudden evaporation of their bravery; all the more bitter the shame of their desertion. What empty words of promise; yet who among us doesn't own a history spoiled with the litter of broken promises?

Like those frightened eleven, it is not the promises we keep that save us, it is the promise God keeps; we are delivered by mercy, not by merit. That is a lesson we learn over and over again, rehearsing it every Good Friday, renewing it in every confession of sin, reclaiming it in every act of worship. We don't need bravery to be saved, certainly not bravado. We need God.

I lay my sins at your feet, Lord Christ, and you place on my head the crown of forgiveness.

SATURDAY EVENING
READING: MARK 14:32–36

"Not what I will, but what thou wilt."

I need these four verses as desperately as I need any in Scripture; Jesus is so redeemingly human in this episode in Gethsemane. In the face of death, he is afraid. How tempted Mark must have been to soften this stark disclosure. There were exaggerations he had allowed to creep in; five thousand is surely more than were fed on that hillside, why not sweeten this episode a little? Or, better yet, leave it out altogether?

But Mark resists these editorial opportunities; he tells it just as it came to him: "horror and dismay" came over Jesus. He did not want crucifixion, he did not want death. Out of the depths of a vital and virile manhood came his plea: "take this cup away from me." So plain, so desperate, so human.

Years ago, Harry Emerson Fosdick wrote a book about Jesus called *The Manhood of the Master;* the truth of that title is never out of place. Jesus is a person, undiminished and inviolate in his humanity, flesh of our flesh, frailty of our frailty. He goes to his death with dignity and decision, but only after a struggle of the most intense emotional reality. We dare not lose the depth of his resistance in the nobility of his resolution. His affirmation is heroic: "Not what I will, but what thou wilt." But it came at the end, not at the beginning; it does not open his prayer, it closes it.

The opening of the prayer reaches out across the whole span of human history and speaks for every created soul in its resistance to this final, fatal obedience. So does the closing of the prayer fold every man, woman, and child in its redeeming embrace and seal forever our power to claim our destiny in the power by which he claimed his.

You have walked the way from resistance to resolution, Lord Jesus; walk with us as we tread, again and again, that stony path.

PALM SUNDAY MORNING
READING: MARK 14:37–42

"Were you not able to stay awake for one hour?"

The eleven slept through it all. It is as Jesus said, "The spirit is willing but the flesh is weak"; he created no truer or more memorable aphorism. But I take the sleep of the disciples more as trust in him than as weakness of the flesh. After all, one doesn't fall asleep when he's scared to death; surges of adrenalin are hardly soporific. What must have enabled their sleep was the reassurance of his demeanor, his outward calm. That power of presence which stilled the storm stilled also their anxious restlessness; his withdrawal into prayer left them confident and quieted. The dark trauma of this night would be vividly etched in their memories; their slumber at this point has something childlike and appealing about it.

The time of trial ends with Jesus in command. "Up, let us go forward!" There is resolution and decision in that summons: "I will not be taken like a cornered fugitive." Jesus has chosen his fate and everything about his voice and posture reveals it; no cowering victim he, but one who has wrestled and won; one who has bared the last dark corner of his self-will and chosen the light.

Every early morning in the lonely place of prayer has counted in that choice; every searching meditation, every sudden plea for grace, every disciplined quiet, every spontaneous recollection— each weighs in the force he brings to that decision. He is bold and commanding; years of daily preparation shape the stride that takes him to this fatal encounter.

We would imitate your courage and your resolve, Lord Jesus; help us imitate your daily discipline of prayer and preparation.

PALM SUNDAY EVENING
READING: MARK 14:43–50

"Judas . . . appeared, and with him a crowd armed."

The futility of arms! This scene is particularly preposterous: Jesus—who has led a parade, has outraged the Temple merchants, has frequented the markets and squares of Jerusalem all this week and all defenseless—is now advanced upon in the dead of night by a faceless mob with swords and cudgels. It's like a scene from comic opera, these brave defenders of righteousness hiding behind their anonymity and their overkill—comic but for the terror all night riders bring with them.

I wonder if arms ever really change anything. The hopes that greeted the end of World War II soon foundered in the chill of the Cold War that replaced it; and only a balance of nuclear terror maintains the tenuous and fragile peace that prevails today. The policy has been called Mutually Assured Destruction and its acronym, MAD, is mordantly prophetic and cautionary. Arms in the service of spirit are no more effective than arms resisting it; note the irony and futility in Mark's description of the sword raised in Jesus' defense—he cut off an ear.

"Then all deserted and ran away." That sounds like the last of them, doesn't it, like the final word. No more than the word of Jesus' burial was the last word of him, is this the final word about the eleven. No, we will hear from them. "Greater things will you do," he promised and, indeed, their part of the New Testament is larger than his.

So, too, with us; he holds our place open for us. For all our infidelity, he keeps pursuing us, calling us back, giving us another chance.

Your love left you defenseless, Holy Jesus; strengthen in us the love that needs no weapon and fears no assault.

Study Aids VI

These discourses of Jesus before the final conflict are heavily laden with Church themes; they have to do with the fellowship of God's people and the institutional life that attaches to that community. He speaks of entrenched leadership, of the collection of money, of the impermanence of all things human. In chapter 13, the little apocalypse, his dominant theme is cautionary: do not be misled, be alert, be forewarned. He speaks of the end of the world in catastrophic terms and leaves the impression it may be soon.

Chapter 14 introduces the Passion narrative, the first sequence of the Gospel story to be committed to writing. Indications are that Mark expanded and perhaps rearranged the material he depended on; each of the Gospels tells it a little differently. Jesus' enemies begin to plot in earnest, Judas arranges his betrayal; we watch this band of men at their final supper together and Jesus in his decisive wrestling with his destiny.

SUGGESTIONS FOR DISCUSSION AND REFLECTION:

How faithful to the Gospel are our fund-raising efforts? (12:41–44, also 10:17–27, 8:34–9:1)

Jesus mentions the Holy Spirit only three times: 3:29, 12:36, 13:11. Does this surprise you?

What do we believe about the Second Coming?

Can you account for the disciples' fury at Jesus' anointing? (14:3–9)

Why do you suppose Judas betrayed Jesus? What did he betray? (14:10–11)

The early church's reenactments of the Last Supper were an authentic meal, more like a church supper than a service of worship. Should we restore that primitive practice? (14:22–25)

What options were open to Jesus in the garden of Gethsemane? Was it necessary that he die? (14:32–42)

Thinking back over your reading of Mark, what would you say is Jesus' view of sin: Is it rebellion? Ignorance? Social? Individual? Is there such a thing as enlightened self-interest? Does the Church sin?

HOLY WEEK

MONDAY MORNING
READING: MARK 14:51–52

"He slipped out of the linen cloth and ran away naked."

Look carefully at these verses; trained literary woodsmen find here the footprints of Mark himself. The Gospels are all anonymous; they carried originally neither title nor author. No internal evidence identifies the authors; even the fourth Gospel is highly indirect in pointing to John as its source. The names were attached early but without much more than pious conjecture or the thinnest testimony: "Papias says that the Elder says . . ." Those early titles were quaint and cryptic: "according to Mark," "according to John," was all they said.

Perhaps a becoming modesty moved the evangelists to let their words stand on their own merits without authentication by the reputation of an author. Like John the Baptist, they saw their purpose as pointing to Jesus, focusing all attention on him, elevating him and his saviorhood at the expense of any pride of authorship or notoriety by association. But there is no narrative purpose served by these verses, no addition to our knowledge of Jesus, no heightened dramatic impact.

What can it be but that in his own human way Mark is loathe to leave himself out altogether? Like the tiny impression struck by the silversmith on an unimportant surface of his artifact, Mark has left his small identifying impression on his gift. Since he is revealing a particularly determined apostasy, I believe we can forgive him.

Forgive our fears and frailties, Lord; our flight measures the tenor of the moment, not the possibilities of the future.

MONDAY EVENING
READING: MARK 14:53–54

"Peter followed him at a distance."

True to his impetuous nature, Peter fell in at the rear of the procession which tramped through the night to the high priest's house, its captive in tow. Right into the courtyard he went, thinking to lose himself in the crowd. We've got to admire Peter for that; his flight wasn't complete. He can't bring himself to desert completely, so, without plan or purpose, he follows Jesus at a distance.

So like us. We're in and we're not in; we surrender and we don't surrender; we can't quite stand with Jesus in the face of terror, but we can't quite cut ourselves loose from him either. Like Peter we follow at a distance, our discipleship undermined by indecision, our obedience inconstant and fickle. I guess I don't know any other kind of Christian. The Book of Revelation is rather hard on us; to the church in Laodicea, the Spirit says, "You are neither hot nor cold . . . I will spit you out of my mouth." The Prayer Book is kinder; it bids us confess our perfidy and accept God's forgiveness. That forgiveness is sealed by the very events transpiring in the dark stealth of this courtyard, where one man is faithful and another is not.

But a word for Peter: he was there. When Jesus caught sight of him, I wonder if he didn't think: Yes, Peter will abandon me; but it is like him to follow a little further than the others.

———————————

We are disciples with dragging feet, Lord Jesus; help us, like Peter, to stay at least in sight of you.

TUESDAY MORNING
READING: MARK 14:55–65

"Many gave false evidence against him."

Lawyers with a biblical bent have studied this trial to discover its congruency with the Jewish legal standards of the time. They are hampered by simple lack of evidence of the practices of the era. When Jerusalem was leveled in A.D. 140, in response to a major rebellion, the destruction included the kinds of documents and records that could have shed light on the ecclesiastical jurisprudence of Jesus' time.

But the Gospels make a plain, if imprecise, case for a miscarriage of justice: witnesses in disagreement, prosecutors fishing for a sustainable offense, patently false evidence paraded before the court. Through it all, a sense of calm at the center, a sense of Jesus in control, impassive while they fumble at the appearance of justice, letting their hasty plot run its futile course. The victim quietly commands the scene; their frustration swirls around him, his presence an aggravation to their impatience and the crumbling of their hollow case. For all the planning and plotting, the scurrying and the scheming, it is the character of Jesus that shapes these events, his personality is the fulcrum on which they turn.

Jesus breaks his silence only to convict himself; unresponsive to the piecemeal evidence, he answers directly the one direct question addressed him. "Are you the Messiah?" "I am." The blazing irony of that conviction! That the nation so long awaiting the arrival of Messiah, so long focusing its life and institutions on his coming, should make it a crime to claim to be him. A foolish exaggeration, perhaps, a dismissable pretense, maybe, a laughable absurdity—but a capital crime? How could the Messiah announce his arrival if such a claim were blasphemy on its face? How could the Messiah disclose himself if such revelation were a hanging offense by definition?

Thus does religion defeat its own purposes by fear of its own truth; thus does religion rule its own Master and conceal the reality of God by making his house his prison.

Remind us, O God, that your reality is in you and not in our definitions, that your truth is in your action and not in our response.

TUESDAY EVENING
READING: MARK 14:66–72

"I do not know this man you speak of."

History. There is this undeniability about it, this inerasable, indelible quality of it. It's there: stark, sure, heavy with reality, freighted with consequence. Here, in these six verses, part of Peter's life is writ forever in the stones of time, never to be altered, never to disappear. Like every human episode, the narrative of life flows through it and is forever different because of it.

That truth would be the doom and damnation of all of us if it weren't for the equally durable and unchangeable fact of redemption, the strange and unreasonable fact of our capacity to build good lives on bad history, even to build better lives on bad history. That third chapter of Genesis records the most startling and far-reaching mutation of the whole long history of God's creation: we left the paradise of perfection for the mystery of morality. The mystery of choice, freedom, consequence, responsibility, redemption—no consistent philosophy can embrace that range of truth because we haven't found the language that can contain that explosive wonder. We can't undo history; it's gone and we can't go back. But we can redeem it, we can build good out of it, we can transform what is ugly and despicable into what is radiant and lovely. Like Good Friday, when the hand of God seized the ultimate evil and shaped it into the ultimate good. It is a most awesome alchemy by which God empowers us to make golden lives out of leaden sin, but it is what we mean by all those Gospel imperatives that summon us to the future: repent, believe, take up, come, follow.

Those bitter tears of shame that Peter shed will, wonder of wonders, be made a fountain of new life, and he and God will fashion, out of the wreckage of this night, a life of grace and power.

The grandest miracle of all, O God, is your power to bring good out of evil; set that power to work in my life and in the life of every person.

WEDNESDAY MORNING
READING: MARK 15:1–15

"So Pilate, in his desire to satisfy the mob, handed him over to be crucified."

Of course it is Pilate who is really on trial here. Every time a person is haled before the bar of justice, the court is on trial along with the accused. And not the court only, but the whole society, its values, its expression of those values in laws, and its entire law-enforcement apparatus. All this is tested and revealed in our dealing with the offender: What are his rights? How is he treated? What are the procedures, the punishments, the remedies? Every time the bailiff announces the solemnities of justice, both sides—accused and accuser, criminal and court, offender and society—are tested.

Pilate flunked. The judgment of history on this trial is plain: the Son of God goes on to his ministry of sacrifice and salvation; the governor enters history as the man who executed him. Pilate saw the farce and mockery of the whole tawdry business; but the mob had its way. So Roman justice, the pride of the ancient world and a model for our own, failed in the hands of a weak man.

But Pilate tried. He sought the alternative of Passover amnesty, he shouted back at the crowd. So much of the story is one of good intentions that collapsed, courage that couldn't reach far enough. Peter, and now Pilate. I have thought if Pilate had stuck it out, if he had turned away the mob and sent them on to seek another cover for their lynching, he would have forfeited his place in history and his infamy would have settled on whoever finally gave the fraudulent sanction. Pilate's noble tenacity, his stern defense of justice would have been forgotten, lost in the dust of memory along with most human heroism. He would have entered the Kingdom as one of those last promised to be first, rather than leaving it as one of those first doomed to be last.

Add tenacity to our faith, dear God; life will test our trust and without your strength we fail.

WEDNESDAY EVENING
READING: MARK 15:6–21

"So Pilate released Barabbas."

Uprisings were fairly common events in Jerusalem at Passover time; apparently from such an ill-fated outburst the chief priests had selected Barabbas as beneficiary should Pilate offer the release of a prisoner. We know nothing more about him or his gesture of patriotism; conjecture has focused on the effect this unexpected substitution might have had on the direction of his life. There is ancient manuscript evidence that his name was Jesus Barabbas and that Pilate was asking which Jesus they wanted, the rebel or the king? I am fascinated by his surname because it means "son of the father," so like the name of deity we have given Jesus, and so like the destiny we claim for all mankind.

Another minor actor walks across the stage and disappears: Simon of Cyrene, apparently seized as a bystander, a Jew handy to the brutality of a foreign soldier, a fit beast for an onerous burden and a footnote of humiliation for the instruction of any rebellious spirits among the onlookers. But again, appearances are deceiving. It turns out it was Jesus who seized Simon; what looked like the random selection of a Roman soldier proved to be the subtle work of an unsleeping Providence. Look back at the path Simon trod in this drama and we see two sets of footprints: those of Rufus and Alexander.

The sudden weight pressed on his shoulders becomes, for Simon, the occasion of his meeting God. It's an old story and one we tell again and again: a harsh and senseless adversity is a glove on the hand of God, the darkness of a sorrow is the shadow of his presence. So God takes the mixed, by-chance stuff of the moment and works it patiently into his plan.

We walk this way of pain with you, Holy Jesus; make it for us, as for you, the way of light and victory.

THURSDAY MORNING
READING: MARK 15:22–24

"He was offered drugged wine, but he would not take it."

Golgotha. Its location is lost in archeological uncertainty, but its name is testimony to the grim purpose of the place. The taking of a human life—even in those eras we consider brutal and insensitive—was a sordid business, basically repulsive despite its morbid fascination. It left a sour taste and the naming of this hill "the place of the skull," while doubtless serving as warning, also testifies to that in us that holds life precious and the taking of it a violation of something profound, something deeply essential in the scheme of Creation.

Jesus refused the drug; he had chosen this fate and would not face it in a blurred or shrunken awareness. The heart and hands so given to healing would hardly seek pain for their own sake, but Jesus' role is that of commander rather than victim, and his demeanor must reflect conquest rather than defeat. Crucifixion meant dying by inches. Exposure, pain, physical stress took their torturous toll, until the body could accept no more. Jesus elected to experience this as long as his consciousness held out, and when that failed it was because of the advance of death, rather than the chemistry of drugs.

I see here a paradigm of our own increasing rejection of the heroic measures available for the extension of life. Like Jesus, we don't seek pain for its own sake, but we reject the indignities of tubes and pumps that reduce us to machines, that keep only the mechanisms of life in motion after the individual has expired. It is a thorny and complex issue, but we raise it because we believe the death that machinery can postpone is not our ultimate enemy, but only an episode of awesome transition, monitored and mastered by a waiting God.

We watch with you this hour of suffering, dear Lord, awed by the weight and the granduer of this event.

THURSDAY EVENING
READING: MARK 15:25–32

"The king of the Jews."

The wording of this sign reeks with irony, and the intimidating import of its location over a tortured man would not be lost on the passerby. This king is not accorded even the protocol of his own execution but shares his martyrdom with two common thieves. The world hardly slowed down for the event and the little company that gathered counted more taunters and jesters than friends. Peter's confession comes to mind as a precursor of this scene, where something was perceived as immense by only a few and dismissed as preposterous by everyone else.

The coarse attempts at humor would amuse only the brotherhood that had engineered this lynching. In their bloated satisfaction with themselves, they cannot see the dark fate that is bearing down on them. No coming down from the cross would persuade them, and they know it; that's a lame, self-serving joke. Signs never work, anyway; God simply will not coerce the unwilling heart. Signs are seen by the eyes of faith; they are visible to no other.

There is a meanness that abuses the defenseless; that cowers in the shadows, lusting for conquest but leaving the risk and the nastiness to others. When the outcome is certain, such steal onto the scene and inflate their limp egos on the dirty work of others. I count their presence no light burden for the dying Jesus; something splendid in his manhood must have suffered specific revulsion at the barking of these jackals. It all looks vain and bootless to us but, for him, it laid new torment onto the anguish of exhaustion and defeat.

We look on your helplessness, dear Jesus, only to learn of our sin; we learn of our sin, Lord Christ, only to claim your love.

FRIDAY MORNING
READING MARK 15:33–39

"My God, my God, why hast thou forsaken me?"

The cry of desolation rang out across that hillside; perhaps across the wall and into the borders of the city. I've never been very impressed with the appeal that Jesus gave voice to only the despairing part of a psalm that goes on to confidence and reassurance. Nothing could be more natural than that the songs of his people would come back to him and that he would seek solace in their poetry and their associations. But I cling to the conviction that Jesus did touch the edge of hopelessness, that he was overwhelmed by a sense of isolation and utter loneliness. I believe it related deeply to his manhood and to the humanity you and I share with him.

I believe he had no resource of faith and trust that you and I don't have, and that his crucifixion had for him, therefore, an element of senseless and capricious absurdity. His sure grasp of death as his destiny was assaulted again and again by the insanity of what was happening to him and by the yawning contradiction between his claims and his fate. He had no rock-hard, guaranteed, impenetrable security; he had only his faith and God's will as he understood it, as he had perceived it and heard it and obeyed it. It was a leap for him, and a leap into darkness, just as it is for you and me. Uncertainty awaited on the other side of his decisions, just as it does for us. Risk was a part of his commitment as it is a part of ours. He couldn't *know*, he could only believe. His better obedience brought him a better faith, and his better faith brought him a better assurance; but certainty, no. That lies forever beyond the grasp of knowledge, forever in the realm of trust.

So this cry of abandonment at the brink of death, wrung from the depths of his humanity, where, like us, he must walk into that shadowed valley alone with his faith.

Remembering you were desolate, Lord Jesus, we can bear desolation; touching, as you did, the borders of despair, we take strength from this memory.

FRIDAY EVENING
READING: MARK 15:40–41

"A number of women were also present, watching from a distance."

The women watched from a distance, where they have been relegated by a male society until very recently. I write in a room decorated by a 1937 photograph of the steps of the church I serve, taken after the Good Friday service; it is peopled almost entirely by women. It is no coincidence that two Good Fridays, nineteen centuries apart, would find faithful women gathered to watch with him, to share his pain, to make their fearless witness. The first parish I served had been without a resident priest for forty-two years; it would have died any number of times without its women, without the fidelity of one generation of women that raised another to carry on. They have waited so long to come into their own.

There is a peculiar grace in human presence, a grace that is independent of any particular words said or services performed. An eloquent man of our times endured an agonizing ordeal of hours spent alone, waiting to be badgered with questions, then faced with hostile testimony, then confronted with accusing evidence, after each period on the stand to be ushered back into his isolation. He wrote later that his heart cried out for the company of another person, just to be with him; not to say anything or do anything or offer anything except his presence, the ministry of his just being there. Every clergyman has spent some of his best hours outside surgical suites or emergency rooms, or in undertakers' parlors or police stations, precisely in the role of a supporting presence.

These faithful women, clustered at the edge of this disaster, kept their silent sentinel, and made their mute witness. What they were accomplishing they probably could not have articulated. Why they had come, they probably could not say. The ancient compulsions of love to respond, its ancient urge to support—these are reason enough.

We watch your death, O Lord, mute and helpless; we bring nothing to your hill of suffering but our silence and our pain.

SATURDAY MORNING
READING: MARK 15:42–47

"Then he laid him in a tomb."

The third pivotal stranger enters the Passion narrative; he comes out of obscurity with credentials of prominence, piety, and courage; he returns to it when his mission of burial is accomplished and is heard from no more. Burial. So many attempts have been made to bury Jesus and they all end like Joseph's. He won't stay buried.

I once spoke with a colleague about Jesus having been "enshrined" in the creed; he replied, "Don't you mean entombed?" Enshrined or entombed, we can't keep him boxed in. No definition will hold him, no formula will enclose him; no orthodoxy can exhaust him, no community can own him. He bursts every boundary we establish for him, he escapes every snare that would hold him still. He is like his own description of the spirit: a wind we hear and feel, a breath we cannot tame or capture. He is life, as he said, and life cannot be contained or comprehended.

There is a sad finality in Mark's words, "he . . . rolled a stone against the entrance." But earth's finalities are not God's and this is not the last word of Jesus. The sigh of relief that went round the Temple, the sigh of sorrow from this burial party—both were premature. From Jesus came the first word of Creation—he will speak the last.

Burst, strong Son of God, the tombs of cant and convention we build for you; remind us it is we who are yours, not you who are ours.

SATURDAY EVENING
READING: MARK 16:1–8

"He has been raised again; he is not here."

So essential is the ending of this story, it could have been written on the day of Creation. So deeply annealed into the stuff of life is the reality of grace, Jesus simply had to rise from death, he had to conquer the grave. His life had to break the bondage of death, or faith and hope and beauty and goodness would be all folly, brave and futile voices raised in the cruel and empty darkness. God is not entropy, reality does not run down and disappear into a black hole without memory or meaning. Love had to make this conquest; life had to win this victory.

Still the empty tomb took them utterly by surprise; words can scarcely capture their trembling and dumbfounded astonishment. For all the necessity we see now, the Resurrection was incredible to them. It left them reeling, their recollections of its specifics confused, their records of its particulars conflicting. Mark has them flee in terror, saying nothing, when his record ends abruptly mid-sentence. We are never quite prepared for God's capacity to surprise us; try as we may, we never really learn that we cannot domesticate him, we cannot break him to the halter of our understanding, we cannot predict him.

What countless surprises do you suppose Jesus has yet in store for us?

Accept our thanks, dear Heavenly Father, for the matchless gift of Jesus; we rise up to bless and praise your holy name and to offer ourselves in the service of his kingdom.

Study Aids VII

The denouement. The whole Gospel has been prelude to these swift events and Mark relates them in his sparest narrative style. First before the high priest, where Jesus convicts himself by his fidelity and, oddly enough, Peter convicts himself by his cowardice. Then to Pilate for the execution order, where the governor hesitates. On to the final hill, where history changed forever; then to the tomb and Mark's truncated account of the Resurrection.

So quickly does triumph succeed disaster that his followers are staggered. So do we stagger still, all these generations later, when we try to fashion our lives into an appropriate response.

SUGGESTIONS FOR DISCUSSION AND REFLECTION:

Do you think Jesus expected to return to earth quickly? (14:62) Could the Resurrection be the return of which Jesus spoke?

Would the Church today receive Jesus differently from the Church of his own time?

Is there a difference between being blamed for our sins and taking responsibility for our behavior?

How important is the Resurrection to your faith?

How much does faith depend on accurate theology? On accurate history?